D0279067

Widely hailed as Scotland's most successful football manager since Jock Stein, Alex Ferguson's achievements with Aberdeen Football Club are unparalleled, creating and consolidating a new force in British and European football. Since joining the Dons in 1978, the ambitious, hard-driving and controversial 'Fergie' has seen his side capture eight major trophies — The European Cup-Winners' Cup, European Super Cup, three Scottish Premier League titles and three Scottish Cups.

In *A Light In The North* Alex Ferguson tells for the first time the story the fans have been waiting for.

A LIGHT IN THE NORTH:
SEVEN YEARS WITH ABERDEEN

A LIGHT IN THE NORTH
Seven Years with Aberdeen

by

Alex Ferguson

MAINSTREAM
PUBLISHING

Copyright © Alex Ferguson, 1985
All rights reserved

First published in 1985 by
MAINSTREAM PUBLISHING COMPANY (EDINBURGH) LTD.
7 Albany Street
Edinburgh EH1 3UG

ISBN 1 85158 007 7 (cloth)
ISBN 1 85158 008 5 (paper)

No part of this book may be reproduced or transmitted in any form or
by any means, mechanical or electric, including photocopy, recording or
any information storage and retrieval system now known or to be
invented, without permission in writing from the publisher, except by a
reviewer who wishes to quote brief passages in connection with a review
written for insertion in a magazine, newspaper or broadcast.

Photographs courtesy of Sports Projects.
Cover design by James Hutcheson.

Typeset in 11 point Garamond by Studioscope in conjunction with
Mainstream Publishing.
Printed by M & A Thomson Litho Ltd, East Kilbride.

For Cathy and My Mother

Contents

Introduction

THE MOTIVATION for writing this book didn't come easily. Friends had been prompting me and I'd been pondering over the idea for quite a while. A few publishers were also encouraging me to do an autobiography but my feelings were that it was still too early for that. When someone suggested that I should simply record the story of my seven years as manager of Aberdeen Football Club, that had more appeal.

The final decision was taken on a May night in 1985, at the end of a long, hard season. The double occasion was the BP Youth Cup Final at Pittodrie and the presentation to the club of the Scottish Premier League Championship Trophy by David Letham. The game was to feature Celtic's youth team against Aberdeen's — a truly fitting climax as the senior players of both clubs had battled each other for the League all season. Now it was the chance for the young ones.

I was more excited by the prospect of the match than by any presentation. It was a time for examination of our youngsters, a time to judge progress, assess character and temperament and, more importantly, ability against more publicised opponents. And I was not disappointed. It was the best youth game I've ever seen, played with all the enthusiasm and innocence that only young players can exhibit. As both sets of players abandoned their inhibitions the game reached a frightening standard.

Celtic deservedly led 2-0 at half-time and as I walked towards the dressing room I contemplated what attitude I should take to the lads. Should I be angry or low-key? Not for the first time the old adage that a manager really earns his money at half-time ran through my mind. I decided I wanted to know what these lads were really made of and I let them know that Aberdeen FC expected more from the talent that was sitting there. If they froze on a big occasion as youth team players then what chance had they as first team players performing in front of a crowd of 60,000 in a Cup Final against the likes of Celtic? Finally I made the point that apart from the 6,500 people at Pittodrie that night to see the future of the club, the whole of Aberdeen's first team pool were there. If ever there was a good time for their understudies to let them know just how good they were, this was it!

The second-half was incredible. Celtic took a 3-0 lead but that scoreline was now against the run of play. Our boys were playing some great stuff but just couldn't score. I decided to give our two substitutes — both 15-year-olds — a run for the experience. Suddenly everything went haywire. We got the goal we so richly deserved and the confidence of the boys soared. The game eventually finished 5-3 in our favour after extra-time.

After the young ones had done their lap of honour they were met at the dressing room by the most thunderous welcome. Every player, ground staff member and office staff worker was there to meet them, to backslap and glory in their greatest ever night. Willie Miller went round congratulating each of the lads individually, as did all the club's big names. The sight of that unity moved me. It made me realise that my seven years with the Dons was not the completion of an achievement but only the start. I now felt compelled and totally motivated to record a period of my life which has given me enormous satisfaction and sense of accomplishment, a belief that I've done something really worthwhile.

Chapter One
1978-79: Early Days

THE LAST DAY of May 1978 was not the first time I was asked to manage Aberdeen Football Club. A year previously I had received a phone call from Ally McLeod suggesting I become his successor as he had just accepted the post of Scotland manager. Naturally it was an opportunity which I found difficult to turn down but having played for Ally at Ayr United and respected him, I was able to talk freely to him. Although he was very convincing in his opinion of the club, I finally managed to explain to him that I was trying to make St Mirren, where I was manager, another Aberdeen. Well, without explaining the insanity of that judgement, I stayed with St Mirren another year before an opportunity to join the Dons arose again.

This time contact was made with me through one of the most powerful and influential sports writers in Britain, Jim Rodger of the *Daily Mirror*. Jim is a man of the utmost integrity and one you can trust with your life, so when he approached me I knew it was for real. This time there was no way I was turning the job down. Soon I was chatting on the telephone to the man who symbolises Aberdeen Football Club and who has done so much for me since that day, Dick Donald. He immediately invited me to become manager and asked me to come up to Aberdeen the next day. I immediately accepted both offers.

Within a matter of hours I was driving the 150-odd miles to Pittodrie. As I drove my thoughts were all of the challenge ahead of, and the history behind, Aberdeen Football Club. Under Eddie Turnbull as manager they had won the Scottish Cup in 1970. Then Jimmy Bonthrone took over and what a wonderful person he was. Once when we were chatting he told me he had been all set to offer me the position of assistant manager at Aberdeen while I was player-coach of Falkirk — until I was ordered off at Pittodrie in a Scottish Cup tie after an incident with big Willie Young. That and my somewhat controversial reputation of being a radical as chairman of the Players' Union managed to dissuade him. Then, of course, came that man, Ally McLeod, who succeeded Jimmy and turned the whole place upside down. Under Ally the Dons had won the League Cup in 1976. Finally, after a very short apprenticeship at Clyde, Billy McNeill joined Aberdeen as manager. Although he only stayed for a year the team had done really well, narrowly losing out in the League to Rangers and also being defeated in the Scottish Cup Final by the same opponents. Billy, of course, could not resist the call of his beloved Celtic.

So here I was about to take up potentially the best footballing job north of the border. It was obvious that Aberdeen were a respected team but for a man of my ambition that wasn't quite enough. I wanted to create and develop a side that was feared as well as respected.

In the way of all this stood one painfully obvious double-edged factor, a factor that had to be dealt with if any of my ambitions were to be fulfilled. The Old Firm. Rangers and Celtic, as historical statistics point out, were Scottish football. Every now and again a short threat to their predominance would occur but these challenges were rarely sustained. There had been the great Hibs team of the late 1940s and early 1950s with their glittering forward line of Smith, Johnstone, Reilly, Turnbull and Ormond. There was the talented Hearts team of the 1950's with Mackay and Cumming and a front line of Young, Conn, Bauld, Wardhaugh and Crawford. The 1960s brought brief flirtations from Dundee and Dunfermline, with whom I played at the time, and Kilmarnock won the League in 1965, but the real state of play was put into perspective by the fact that Kilmarnock were the last team outside the Old Firm to win the League until Aberdeen broke the stranglehold in 1980. As far as my thinking was concerned, to win anything you had to beat the Old Firm. My ultimate aim was to have an Aberdeen so good that if any other team was going to win anything in Scottish football it was going to have to beat the Dons.

But, for a variety of reasons, events did not turn out too well for me in my first season at Pittodrie. Two aspects of my life away from football occupied a lot of my thoughts, perhaps occasionally at the expense of the team. The first was my father's illness. It was obvious that he hadn't that long to go and I was spending a fair amount of time travelling back and forth to Glasgow to visit him. The second was the prospect of the tribunal still hanging over me from my St Mirren days when the parting of the ways had left much acrimony and rancour.

Anyway, when I took over at Aberdeen I tended to follow the well-trodden path of most managers when they arrive to take over a relatively successful team: I said that I'd no immediate intentions of changing the set-up but I knew I had my own ideas and thoughts on the game. I gradually introduced my own training programmes although we did also rely a lot on the routines devised by Teddy Scott, himself

Jim Leighton

something of a Pittodrie legend. All his training programmes had been built up over the years and were so varied and complete that they included almost all the exercises I would be giving the players anyway. Pre-season training, then, was a success and I was pleased with the performance and effort by the players. We rounded the programme off with a visit to Gordonstoun — my first chance to go up there although the team had been spending time there since the days of Ally McLeod. It was an environment the players enjoyed and I particularly appreciated it for the simple reason that it was a bit Spartan: it got us all out of the way of the public attention and gave us the ideal opportunity to be together and prepare for the new season.

Our first game under my managership was a friendly against Tottenham Hotspur, who had just signed Ardiles and Villa. The two Argentinians were supposed to be playing at Pittodrie but didn't make it because of a clearance hold-up with their papers. We won 3-1 with an excellent performance. Particularly pleasing was Joe Harper's goal, a real cracker. Unfortunately Bobby Clark broke a knuckle while punching the ball clear. He was obviously going to be out for a few weeks and that made me confront my first real decision — which of our reserve goalkeepers to call in, John Gardiner or a young boy we had just brought in from Deveronvale, Jim Leighton. In training I was more impressed with Leighton, so I decided to play him in the opening competitive match of the season against Hearts at Tynecastle.

It was a wet day with bad conditions for goalkeepers. The ball would be greasy and come shooting off the surface. The boy had an excellent game and gave a superb display of handling, an attribute that has subsequently become a hallmark of his game. He also proved himself to be brave and strong and there was no doubt in my mind after that match that this was a goalkeeper of the future. We won, despite losing the first goal early on and being under a lot of pressure for most of the first-half. But sometimes fortune plays the right part in events. We scored a lucky goal when a long shot from Steve Archibald skidded in underneath the goalkeeper's body. From there we went on to a convincing 4-1 victory and a good start to the season.

After that Tynecastle game our run of success continued until we had gone seven matches in a row without defeat. But to some extent that very success helped me to shy away from making important changes in the way the team were playing. I was seeing signs of weaknesses on the park which did not convince me that this was a real title-winning team or a particularly successful side. The one area which worried me most was the way the team seemed to like to defend in depth, with almost everyone in their own penalty box. It was ultimately negative and potentially suicidal. I was looking for them to defend further up the park, for the midfield men to move out against opponents and not pack the penalty box. Packed penalty areas often meant conceding penalty kicks under stiff challenges from the opposition.

I saw those weaknesses but the combination of our successful run and my personal problems at that time allowed me to let them pass. The one thing I needed, I kept telling myself, was just to get through that first season and then to have time to recharge, to gather myself, to sit down and analyse both myself and the team. Win or lose, a manager must always look at himself and ask, 'What was my contribution?' I think I can honestly say that my contribution that season was less than it should have been. It seems strange to say it now but the Alex Ferguson of that season was not the same Alex Ferguson who had been with St Mirren or East Stirling or who was manager at Pittodrie in subsequent years. I did not make the right decisions, nor did I make them early enough. Two particular lessons I learned that year, however, did stick with me after the season was long since over.

The first occurred on our first match with one of the Old Firm under my management, a League match against Rangers at Ibrox, just after we had lost our unbeaten run to Marek Dimitrov in the European Cup-Winners' Cup over in Bulgaria, where Willie Garner had broken his leg, and after we had suffered our first domestic defeat of the season against Hibs at Easter Road. I remember it was a windy, dirty day in Glasgow as we played in front of a Copland Road stand which was still under construction. At the end we lost to a penalty kick awarded by referee Hugh Alexander — one of many controversial decisions given in that game. But before the game I had been listening to some of the Aberdeen players in the dressing room. They were talking about slowing the game down, taking time at throw-ins and free-kicks so that the notoriously fickle and impatient Ibrox crowd would turn against their own team if they didn't score. I just couldn't understand that philosophy. I wanted to go to Ibrox to beat them. How about letting them worry about us? It was an attitude that disappointed me and I mentally pencilled that in as something that would need to be sorted out.

A second lesson began to be learned that year over the two legs of our second round European Cup-Winners' Cup tie with Dusseldorf. One of the early mistakes I made as a manager was made there *after* the first-leg game which we lost 3-0. We came back to the hotel after the game and I expected the players just to go to their beds. Instead a lot of them went nightclubbing — a jaunt I made sure was never going

17

to be repeated, especially midweek with an important match coming up on the Saturday. Almost predictably, we came back after the Dusseldorf game and lost at home to Hearts. Stuart Kennedy was taken off injured in the first few minutes and we were caught short of adequate defensive cover. I ended up having to play Dom Sullivan at right-back, where the lively and elusive Denis McQuade gave him a real hard time. Towards the end of the game McQuade cut in and hit a screamer of a shot 30 yards into the corner of the net to beat us 2-1.

That was a black period. There were all sorts of stories and rumours about the town about the players not accepting me. In fact I remember the local paper speculating the morning after the Dusseldorf return match about things not being quite right at Pittodrie, how the players were not responding to the manager. It carried interviews with supporters about their attitudes to what was going on, as well as interviews with the chairman and Willie Miller. Quite frankly it was disappointing. It made me a wee bit more resilient because if nothing else I react to adversity. It made me grit my teeth and that saw me through a bad period.

In that return match with Dusseldorf I was keen to put Gordon Strachan into the team but rather than create even more controversy at a difficult time I played Dom Sullivan from the start of the match. I did decide to bring Bobby Clark back in as a gamble despite the fact that he had played the night before against Arbroath Reserves. As usual, Bobby didn't let us down. In fact it was an excellent Aberdeen performance. We managed to beat Dusseldorf 2-0 and still missed all sorts of chances, hitting the post, hitting the bar, hitting everything but the stand. We still went out 3-2 on aggregate.

But our experiences that year taught us a few lessons about Europe — about patience, about playing away from home and not giving the ball away. We started to learn, there is no doubt about that. Perhaps more important was that the European stage had allowed me to introduce Gordon Strachan and he was marvellous.

Of course there are also other highlights that season. We had a marvellous tactical performance against Celtic in my first confrontation with Billy McNeill's team. The fact that Billy had been manager at Pittodrie before me helped to introduce an intensity which was at times unhealthy. He always took defeat badly and so did some of his players and that led to some heated confrontations in the tunnel after our games. That was a pity because the fact remains that we were in the game to win too. But it's now a fact of life they have to recognise as part of the Scottish football scene — Aberdeen are here to stay.

Before that first clash with Celtic I had sent Pat Stanton to see

Pat and I

19

them play in a midweek match while we were at Hamilton in a League Cup tie. Pat felt that the young left-back, Sneddon, lacked experience and could be drawn towards the ball, and that the centre-backs McDonald and Edvaldsson did not like to get out to wide areas. Pat had played in that position and knew what he was talking about. Now, before that game I had dropped Dom Sullivan from a few matches because he would not conform to the way I liked a midfield player to play, but I felt he could play a part in this game because of his stamina and his ability to make runs off the ball. He would be useful in playing against Tommy Burns. We decided to play Gordon Strachan out wide and forward to try to draw Sneddon towards the ball and to let Archibald run into the areas behind Sneddon, against Edvaldsson or McDonald, with Joey Harper operating through the middle. We won 4-1 and could have scored two or three more. It was a good start for me in my confrontations with Celtic and also good for the sport in that after so many battles with Big Billy as a player, here I was rekindling the rivalry.

We also reached the League Cup Final that season. On our way there we met Ayr United who were now managed by the irrepressible Ally McLeod. We played them at Somerset Park and Steve Archibald was sent off by referee Brian McGinlay after an incident involving the Ayr goalkeeper. I always felt that Brian McGinlay was not one of Archibald's greatest fans. Steve never got an inch off him and this led indirectly to a confrontation between Brian and myself later on in an incident at Easter Road the day we won the League — a confrontation that earned me a year's ban! After the sending-off we managed to scramble a 3-3 draw and then beat them 3-1 at Pittodrie in the return.

In the semi-final of that League Cup we beat Hibs, who were managed by Eddie Turnbull, another former Aberdeen manager. It seemed I was having my share of confrontations with my Aberdeen predecessors, but Turnbull was very different from Ally or Big Billy. I didn't like him at all. He was a sour individual and I was delighted with our 1-0 victory over his team at Dens Park, even if it did go to extra-time. Mike McDonald, their goalkeeper, was unbelievable in that game. He put up the shutters all night, saving shots from Joey Harper twice and then a great header from Neil Cooper (not the one who's with us now, but the one who went to Barnsley and then St Mirren). Eventually, towards the end of the first period of extra time, when we were shooting down the hill again, Stuart Kennedy hit one of his high crosses which big Mike palmed into the net. I couldn't believe my ears when after the game, in the Dens Park boardroom, one Hibs director said McDonald would never kick another ball for them. He was almost true to his word and the big goalkeeper never played many games for Hibs after that.

The League Cup Final itself was postponed until 31 March, by which time we had progressed to the semi-final of the Scottish Cup by way of Hamilton Accies and Ayr United, who were then managed by Willie McLean. In the quarter-finals we were drawn against Celtic. In the Pittodrie game I witnessed possibly the best goal I have ever seen as manager of Aberdeen — scored by the hero of the Aberdeen support and a legend among the Dons fans, Joey Harper. Celtic had just scored, a Burns header, before half-time. We centred the ball and it was rolled back to Kennedy, who knocked it up towards the penalty box. Wee Joey, going down to the Paddock end, running from the South Stand towards the Main Stand, took this ball over his shoulder on the volley from about twenty yards and it roared into the net. It was a helluva goal, one whose equal will not be seen for a long time. But that was typical of Joey, a player who could score out of nothing.

At any rate, we had our 1-1 draw. I now had to decide for the replay whether to play Alex McLeish who played in the first match or Doug Rougvie who missed that game through suspension. I opted for Doug because he was more aggressive. I felt sure he could frighten one or two of them down at Celtic Park. The atmosphere was going to be electric. Alex was young so I opted to use him on the bench.

We got off to a great start in front of a crowd of 50,000, and were 2-0 up before the game had gone on too long. We scored a goal from a free-kick. Duncan Davidson rolled it in. Then goalkeeper Latchford dropped the ball and Steve Archibald scored with a header off a Harper cross. We were on our way. Dom Sullivan was carried off with a shoulder injury following a clash with a Celtic player and I brought on Alex McLeish to man-mark Tommy Burns. He followed him everywhere. He really made a tremendous contribution that night. The game was hectic, there were cans thrown on the park and I remember the scenes were unbelievable but we managed to hang on to a 2-1 win. It was a great moment. Unfortunately there were a lot of incidents inside the tunnel, with the players fighting and officials arguing. Quite frankly, Celtic took it badly. I was really disappointed. It detracted attention from the result but we still managed to celebrate a marvellous victory that got us through to the semi-final.

Before the semi-final could be played we came up against Rangers in that famous League Cup Final. Sullivan still wasn't fit so we played a midfield of Strachan, McMaster and Jarvie. If Sullivan had been fit I would have played a four-man midfield with Strachan, Sullivan, McMaster and Jarvie, but Sullivan's natural replacement, Scanlon, was talking about leaving for America at that time. He had come to see me when we were going through the last preparations for the game and said he didn't want to play, that he was not in the right frame of mind. I was raging. I was really angry with the player but these things happen. I got to know Ian and understood him well. He is not a complex person. He is a little bit nervous and a little bit worked up at times, though basically he is a nice lad and one I have a lot of time for. But as I later found out, he was at times a luxury and one of the most frustrating characters because he had a great balance and could beat a man and turn him inside-out. The thing was he would end up not getting the cross in. It was infuriating and frustrating to me as a manager to watch. He would draw back that beautiful left foot of his and you would be looking for a most delicate and brilliant cross to come in and then, all of a sudden, he would throw the ball back on his right foot and of course all the strikers had to stop and check. They just wouldn't know when the cross was coming in. He was a tremendously talented player and he could get a goal through but I was really disappointed in him on that particular occasion. It put me under a lot of pressure as I didn't have a lot of options. I then decided to play Duncan Davidson along with Steve Archibald and Joey Harper.

In the very first minute of the game a controversial incident took place. One deplorable thing about the game in Scotland is the tackle from the back. In that first minute Derek Johnstone who started the match at centre-half made the most disgraceful tackle on Steve Archibald. Effectively it was the end of Archibald, but in the Cup Final no one is going to get sent off or booked within sixty seconds. Because Ian Scanlon was out at his own request, I was faced with having to play two defenders, Alex McLeish and Neil Cooper, and although I had signed Mark McGhee a few days before the Final I felt it was unfair to use him. Archibald struggled on but he was severely handicapped and this was a major blow to us in that particular game.

It was quite an even match. Rangers were perhaps more on top in the early part of the first-half, but we never had any serious problems. In the second-half we scored with about 25 minutes to go and were looking good, and there was a chance just after that when we could have been two up. For a minute I started to think, 'Is this going to be my first trophy? Are we going to beat Rangers in a Final?' I found myself doing a strange thing — I started to pray. Teddy Scott turned round and saw me and said, 'You don't need to pray, son. We've won it, they are never going to score.' That was the way it was looking. Then Alex Miller got the ball out on the far side of the park at the main stand. We were sitting in the dugout, one of the most difficult places to see from in the whole of Hampden — particularly annoying when your team is under threat. Miller was not the type of player who was going to beat anyone or get to the byeline or do anything brilliant. He was a steady, average player and our left-back, Charlie McLelland, who should have known better, dived at him in a no-man's area where it wasn't going to matter. Alex Miller caught him out and squared the ball to Alex MacDonald. Now just prior to that Bobby Clark had gone down injured and our physio was waiting for the game to stop so that he could get treatment. But before the game could be stopped MacDonald hit a shot that spun off John McMaster's ankle and the ball flew into the far corner, leaving Bobby Clark grasping thin air. It was a terrible blow which in effect lost us the Cup. Although it was only 1-1, Bobby Clark was really toiling, Archibald was struggling, and we were rolling on towards the final minutes. Rangers next scored six minutes into injury time because of the incident which I will now talk about.

At the particular period when we were up 1-0, Rangers never looked like doing anything. Billy Urquhart from Caley was taken off with Johnstone coming up from centre-half as a gamble against Doug Rougvie, who had just been booked by the referee for an obvious challenge on Davie Cooper. While we were attacking, and the referee had his back to the incident, something happened involving Johnstone and Rougvie. I remember that Ian Foote came out in the newspapers after he retired from the game saying that he saw Johnstone being pole-axed and punched in the back. I don't believe him. As far as I am concerned, there is no way that he saw the incident. I have seen it on video and the STV copy of the film and there is no way he could have seen anything. I am convinced to this day that Johnstone played to get the foul and made the most of it. He had a reputation for going under defenders when the ball was in the air and I am sure that he came up against Rougvie and Rougvie shoved him out of the road to go for the ball. Johnstone played it up as much as he could, knowing that Rougvie had been booked, and he went down.

Now to begin with his back was being treated, then it was his neck. He lay there for fully five minutes to get treatment. In essence this cost Rougvie his place in the game. To be sent off in a Cup Final is a terrible blow to any player, particularly when it was an unjustified sending off. I did not see the incident, I cannot claim to have seen it, but what I do know is that the referee did not see it either. I don't believe for one minute that he saw Rougvie and Johnstone clash.

After the game I was raging. I felt something must have happened. But when I verbally attacked Rougvie about it, all the players went to his defence and the boy sat there crying and swore on his mother's life

23

that he did not touch Johnstone. 'Johnstone backed into me,' he said, 'and I pushed him aside to go for the ball because I didn't want to be involved with him.' He knew that he had been booked, he didn't want any more incidents and he was trying to be as careful as he possibly could. He said that Johnstone definitely conned the referee. I believe him. We tried to console him and get him sorted out a little by mumbling platitudes about things being sent to try us, how you've got to show your character and overcome adversity. Inside we were all sick.

That certainly was a day which Doug Rougvie will never forget. I was talking at the press conference afterwards and I said to Pat Stanton, 'For goodness sake, don't let Rougvie out of your sight, because if he gets out there and sees Johnstone, God help him.' Certainly that would have happened if Doug Rougvie had got his hands on Derek Johnstone that day . . . put it this way — Rangers would not have been able to sell him to or buy him back from Chelsea years later.

That was a terrible climax to my first Final as a manager. With 30 minutes to go I felt we had won it and 30 minutes later we were out and we were down. It is a true saying that when you're playing the Old Firm you've never won till the final whistle.

There is no doubt also that finals and games that really matter are the measure of the man. I think it is fair to say that once we got our first success in beating Celtic at Celtic Park that season we improved beyond doubt. For many of the players that certainly was the most important game of their lives because it proved to them that they could beat the Old Firm and they could beat them in front of an atmosphere which was at the very least intimidating. It was the measure of them, it made them men and it made them players of real note. It stood them in good stead in years ahead.

At the end of the day the total summary of my first season as manager was this. We amassed 40 points in the League and ended up fourth but still managed to qualify for Europe. We made it to the League Cup Final and the semi-final of the Scottish Cup.

As I said, the season couldn't come to an end quickly enough. I was desperate to go and re-think and analyse, to assess myself and where I was going and how I should go about it. I knew what I wanted, there is no doubt about that. There was nothing wrong with my ability as a manager. Winning the League did not make Alex Ferguson — what made Alex Ferguson and brought me success at Aberdeen was getting a summer break. Going away to re-think. Coming back into next season. But never once did I doubt my own ability.

Certainly one of the outstanding individuals in the Aberdeen

Bobby Clark and I celebrate

set-up in my first season was Bobby Clark, who in his way was a legend. The fact that he was one of the few who had the proper recognition from the support in his testimonial game, when there was a full house to watch the select game, was proof. It was good to see because he had been a great servant to the club. Bobby is a thoroughly dedicated professional. He never gave a minute's bother and he was one of the players who supported me in my early days at Pittodrie. I will be ever grateful to him.

Stuart Kennedy, whom I had managed as a boy was another strong individual. I brought him into the first team at Falkirk although I had only three months with him before he went on to better things with Aberdeen — he was no bother. Drew Jarvie was another outstanding influence. Most of the old stalwart pros — McLelland, McMaster and that type — were all good men.

I must admit my early start with Willie Miller was not encouraging at all. We had one confrontation, but to be fair to the man he came and apologised and from that moment on I think it was the best thing that happened. We had an 'eyeball to eyeball' which saw it out. I never gave an inch, he never gave an inch. It was almost like OK Corral with guns blazing, but it was the best thing that happened. From that time on Willie Miller and I have formed one of the best relationships a manager and captain could ever have. I now have nothing but admiration for him.

At the end of my first season we transferred Chick McLelland to Motherwell. He was another great little character and gave his all to the club. Chick was a good left-back but many, including myself, would often question the depth of that ability. Eventually the criticisms and reservations began to wear him down, though, and he came to me and asked if he could go. He went on to serve Motherwell for many years.

But Bobby Clark was dedicated and never gave me a minute's worry. A good sound goalkeeper, good organiser, good user of the ball, he played some marvellous games for us. To his detriment, it is his own pride that really cost Bobby Clark his place in football because he was a helluva man for doing weights. When I spoke to him about it he said, 'Look, Peter Shilton used to do these weights.' I said. 'You should write to him and get all his assessments.' I knew that Shilton eventually had to stop excessive weight-training because he was becoming muscle-bound, although it certainly did serve its purpose in making him feel powerful. But Bobby used to lift and push the most amazing numbers of weights and it frightened me to watch him on the machine. In time it did harm him. He got a back injury from which he never fully recovered and eventually, in effect, it put him out of the game. Disappointing, because he had so many years to give to the game and he looked after himself. He didn't smoke, he was a very average social person and only enjoyed the occasional beer.

A true illustration of the affection which the Aberdeen support felt for Bobby Clark was that amazing crowd of 22,000 who turned up for his testimonial the September I arrived at Pittodrie.

But for that back injury Bobby would almost certainly have achieved his ambition of playing until he was 40. Nonetheless he was a first-class player for Aberdeen and held the record for the number of games played for the club until Willie Miller surpassed his tally recently.

He helped me, as I say, in some great games. The one in particular I remember was at Celtic Park the following season. We had beaten them 3-2 at Pittodrie in the League Cup first-leg and then 1-0 away. I remember the game at Celtic Park because in the first-half and part of the second-half they actually bombarded our goal. We had a magnificent game that day and it stands out in my mind, as does one special save in the season we won the League. It was a great piece of goalkeeping. It was also an important save for him because he had won everything except a League Medal. He had been capped 17 times, had Scottish Cup Badges and League Cup Badges, and was always denied the big one.

PREMIER DIVISION CHAMPIONSHIP

	P	W	L	D	F	A	Pts
CELTIC	36	21	9	6	61	37	48
RANGERS	36	18	9	9	52	35	45
DUNDEE UNITED	36	18	10	8	56	37	44
ABERDEEN	**36**	**13**	**9**	**14**	**59**	**36**	**40**
HIBERNIAN	36	12	11	13	44	48	37
ST MIRREN	36	15	15	6	45	41	36
MORTON	36	12	12	12	52	53	36
PARTICK THISTLE	36	13	15	8	42	39	34
HEARTS	36	8	21	7	39	71	23
MOTHERWELL	36	5	24	7	33	86	17

SCOTTISH CUP

Third Round	Hamilton Accies	Away	W	2-0	
Fourth Round	Ayr United	Home	W	6-2	
Fifth Round	Celtic	Home	D	1-1	
Replay	Celtic	Away	W	2-1	
Semi-final	Hibs	Hampden	L	1-2	

LEAGUE CUP

2nd R 1st leg	Meadowbank	Away	W	5-0	
2nd leg	Meadowbank	Home	W	4-0	
3rd R 1st leg	Hamilton	Away	W	1-0	
2nd leg	Hamilton	Home	W	7-1	
Q-final 1st leg	Ayr United	Away	D	3-3	
2nd leg	Ayr United	Home	W	3-1	
Semi-final	Hibernian	Dens	W	1-0	AET
Final	Rangers	Hampden	L	1-2	

EUROPEAN CUP-WINNERS' CUP

1st R 1st leg	Marek Dimitrov	Away	L	2-3	
2nd leg	Marek Dimitrov	Home	W	3-0	5-3
2nd R 1st leg	Fortuna Dusseldorf	Away	L	0-3	
2nd leg	Fortuna Dusseldorf	Home	W	2-0	2-3

Top Scorer: Joe Harper 31

Chapter Two
1979-80: *Winning the League*

FOR OUR pre-season training for the 1979-80 season we had a hard spell at Gordonstoun and had already decided that we would round off the schedule by taking the players over to Randers in Denmark where, like most continental sides, they had tremendous training facilities even though they were a second or third division team at the time. In the close season Brian Scott, our physio, had left to join Billy McNeill at Celtic, so we were obviously quite keen to find a replacement before our Denmark trip.

Roland Arnott, an Englishman, was our choice from the applicants and we had written to him asking him to telephone us as time was running short. I never fully understood how Roland had managed to hear of the job as we had only advertised in Scotland but he was certainly keen to prove his affinity with Scotland and consistently claimed to have a Scottish grandfather. Being English, I warned him when he came up for the interview, he was bound to take a bit of ribbing from the players. At any rate we were impressed by him and glad to have him along on the Danish trip.

The visit to Denmark itself was a great success and the players showed good attitude in training. Inevitably, though, Roland was caught out. One day at lunch there was a long table set out for the players, the directors and myself. I was called away to the telephone and when I came back the chairman leaned over and whispered to me: 'Alex, the players have gone too far now.' 'What's happened?' I asked. 'They've asked Roland to say grace,' he replied. 'As he was a newcomer would he say grace?' And suddenly I was aware of the bold Roland standing up: 'For what we are about to receive . . .' Oh, my God!

So that was Roland, who took some terrible stick for an accident of birthplace, but was a good physio and popular with the players, never more so than when recalling his days as a physio at Wimbledon and providing insight into the great tennis stars. That would have the players in the treatment room engrossed. But I don't honestly think Roland was cut out for football — it was too intense for his nature.

Eventually he was to leave us after the European Cup-Winners' Cup victory and he now works in London. Nevertheless he left behind some fond memories at Pittodrie.

Anyhow, we had a really complete and thorough pre-season preparation, there was a good team spirit about the place and the players were applying themselves really well. I remember making my point to the players on the first day back into training: 'Look, the honeymoon's over. From now on we're going to be doing things the way I want them.' I explained the way I believed the game should be played and how we were going to play that season. It definitely did the trick with the players and I could see a whole change in attitude. But at the end of the day they still needed belief in themselves, they needed to win the games that mattered.

As I said earlier, beating Celtic and Rangers is certainly part of that test of whether you have players that are good enough and whether they have the temperament to win trophies. In my second season with the Dons it went well for us against the Old Firm. In fact we beat each of them twice in two-leg affairs in the League Cup, Rangers first 3-1 at Pittodrie and 2-0 at Ibrox — then Celtic in the quarter final, where we beat them 3-2 at home and 1-0 at Parkhead.

Both of these Celtic matches were memorable for me. In the first Steve Archibald scored a hat-trick and was so delighted. Some of the players encouraged him to keep the ball as a memento of the game. This is the practice of some clubs but not of any under my manager-ship, particularly in this case as I felt that Steve had to be kept firmly under control and not be allowed to get carried away with himself. Next morning I was sitting in Teddy Scott's room when Teddy turned to me and said, 'You'll never believe this but Archibald is away with the ball.' 'Oh, is he?' I said. So when Archibald arrived I hauled him into the office and told him to replace the ball. The following morning, Friday, Pat Stanton, Teddy and I were sitting in a room next to the dressing rooms, having a discussion over a cup of tea, when the door burst open. 'There's your bloody ball!' He booted it hard into the air, ricocheting off three walls and sending us ducking and the teacups flying everywhere. That was Steve.

I also particularly remember that second leg match down at Parkhead for Bobby Clark's superb performance — probably his best ever and certainly the best when he played under me. In the first-half of that game little Joe Harper chased a ball out to the touchline, then just out of nothing he seemed to turn and go down in a heap. It was a serious ligament injury and at a serious time in Joe's career. In many ways it was the beginning of the end of that colourful career. He was

30

carried off and Mark McGhee, whom I had signed the previous Easter, took his place. It had taken Mark a long time to settle in to the Aberdeen set-up and that game at Celtic Park helped him in many ways because he scored the goal that won the game and clinched our semi-final place.

Now, if you beat Rangers and Celtic twice in the League Cup tournament you must be red-hot favourites to lift the trophy. We met Morton in the semi-final at Hampden on a wet and dismal day and went through by 2-1 despite struggling towards the end of the game. However, we reached the Final of the League Cup where our opponents were Dundee United. One of the last times I ever showed indecision as manager of Aberdeen occurred after that first Final.

The game at Hampden ended 0-0 after extra-time, despite Aberdeen's obvious superiority. In fact it was really bad luck that stopped us from winning — I remember one header from Willie Garner sticking in the mud on the goal line and everyone standing watching it. It just lay there with not a soul near it. Willie Miller also had a shot scrape by the post and we missed two or three other chances by hitting the woodwork. Then we were denied a penalty after a diabolical foul in the last three minutes of extra-time when Steve Murray, the former Aberdeen and Celtic player, pulled Drew Jarvie off the ball. When Jim McLean and I spoke after the match he couldn't believe his luck and I knew then he was already deciding what to do in the replay. All credit to the man, he knew he had made a mistake in his choice of team. I swear I could see and feel his relief as well as his determination to make sure the same mistake did not happen a second time. I knew he was going to make changes for that second game.

Well, the indecision I mentioned had more to do with my not making the necessary changes in our team for the second match. I remember saying to Pat Stanton on the bus back to Aberdeen: 'We'll need to change the team. They'll definitely go for four in the middle, I'm certain of that. I've got to think about changing the team, pushing Kennedy up on top of them at one side and maybe McMaster up on the other side, and playing the two centre-backs and Willie Miller at the back.' I was contemplating leaving Willie Garner out, and withdrawing Alex McLeish from centre midfield to centre-half along with Doug Rougvie, to combat Sturrock and Pettigrew who I was sure were going to play as strikers. I wanted Willie Miller free and Stuart Kennedy and John McMaster up in midfield areas with Gordon Strachan playing more as an inside-forward. That Saturday night we had a small reception at Pittodrie but it was a damp squib of a night really. There was no excitement, the players were a bit tired looking and it had been a long journey home.

We gave the players Sunday off and got them in on the Monday to start preparations. I was going to change the team then and get on with it. But that morning Roland Arnott came to see me and said that one of the young players had a fairly serious medical problem. He had gone to the last physio, Brian Scott, and he had recorded it on file but then Brian had left to take up the position at Celtic which meant that nothing was done about it. Of course time had rolled on and the boy was a bit embarrassed to come to the second physio to talk about it. He was expecting to be told that he should go for an examination. Roland thought we should get him up to a specialist right away. We were genuinely worried about him. It was really serious and there was no doubt about that. I just couldn't put my mind on telling the players the line-up for Wednesday's team, so I opted out. I had wanted to list the team as early as possible so I decided to go the easy way, telling them they should have done it in the first game and that the team was good enough to do it in the second. I kept the same team, which was a really bad mistake. It cost us the Cup.

But that Monday morning my mind wasn't on team matters. The lad was whisked straight into hospital for an operation. I was left with the task of getting in touch with his parents to get them up to Aberdeen straight away. His father was travelling on business and his mother answered the phone. I told her we were trying to get in touch with her husband and of course she sensed there was a problem. 'What's wrong?' she asked. I said, 'It's nothing really but perhaps you could get your husand to phone me?' She said she would need to contact his company to find out where he was and I urged her to do so right away. I left it like that and five minutes later she called back and said, 'Look, Mr Ferguson, you're not telling me the truth. There's something wrong. I'm a nurse and I think you should tell me.' So I told her. The company then managed to get in touch with the father and both parents came up to Aberdeen where we put them up in the Atholl Hotel till the whole business was sorted out.

The operation was scheduled for the Wednesday morning, after tests had suggested they should operate as soon as possible. Naturally we were all worried stiff for the boy's sake. The delays were part and parcel of us changing physios but because of that the boy's problem had been left in cold storage. As it turned out he was all right. The operation was successful, and we carried on from there until the boy was able to play again. Now we always stress to the young players at Pittodrie that it is so important that they take advice about problems from me or one of the other training staff at all times.

Anyway the whole episode took my mind off the replay. I was also drained. I remember going down to join the players at Arbroath on the morning of the game and managing a little bit of training before we went to bed in the afternoon.

In the evening the game had been going on just two minutes when I sensed we were going to lose. At the time I was banned from the touchline and I was sitting in the Dens Park stand, a difficult place from which to send anyone down to the track with team messages. I was looking for ways to change the team quickly before United scored, for once they get in front they are really difficult to beat. Eventually we were beaten soundly — 3-0 — on a dirty night at Dens. I really didn't think the Cup was destined for Pittodrie anyway after our missed chances in the first game and the succession of bad luck which continued. But the irony was that we had beaten Rangers and Celtic twice each on the way, while United didn't even meet a Premier League team until the Final itself. We felt that in a way we had done their work for them and yet it was their Cup.

It was a big setback at the time because we had started the season not too badly. I remember we lost the very first game, at Partick, when we had five players missing, including Miller and Kennedy, two of our most experienced men. In the last minute of the game a cross came in from winger Donald Park and big Alex McLeish handled it. So we lost our opening match. We recovered from that and beat Hibs and Dundee United in the following weeks. Then we came up against a team that was really becoming a problem for us — Morton.

It is strange how Morton became our bogey team over the years. They were beating us at Pittodrie despite hardly being in the game. We would have been attacking and attacking them but it still made no difference. They would run up the park and score near the end of the match. In fact the number of times we lost at Cappielow in the last two or three minutes was unbelievable. We tried everything. We sat down with the players and asked, 'Right. How do you want to play?' Unanimously we would agree just to play our normal game. When that still didn't work we tried going down there and playing with only one man up the park in an attempt to draw them forward. But they wouldn't come out, they just sat there defending and defending. We tried playing with two wingers and no strikers, we even tried two wingers and two strikers. We tried playing three at the back. We tried everything, believe me. It wasn't until the last few years that we began to get results.

Of course Morton had some good players like Joe McGlaughlin, Neil Orr, Jim Duffy and the big lad Bobby Thomson. But Andy Ritchie was a large part of the reason we began to get an obsession about them. Andy was always there. He never played particularly well against us but he would always have a go at scoring and his free kicks were often deadly. Once he scored against us from 40 yards and another time from almost the corner flag. He was a thorn in our flesh. I remember during one afternoon coaching session at Pittodrie before a Morton game we even spent time practising the defence in lining up to counteract Andy's free-kicks. But at the end of the day you just couldn't legislate for the lad's magnificent ability in a dead ball situation, particularly, it seemed, against Aberdeen. I can tell you we all breathed a sigh of relief when Andy left Morton!

I remember quite vividly another time we played Morton in the middle of winter. It was snowing and the train bringing them up to Aberdeen broke down. They finally arrived at Pittodrie with only 20 minutes to go before kick-off and we felt sure they'd be in disarray. Surely we'd win this one! We lost 2-1 and Andy Ritchie scored again. Just before they left after the match for the return trip to Greenock I said to Hal Stewart, their chairman, that I hoped their train would break down on the way back as well. Somebody up there must have heard, for reports later came back that their return train spent three hours of a frozen Saturday evening broken down in a siding near Larbert!

Perhaps the most important decision I made that year was on 28 July, right at the start of the season. After a Drybrough Cup tie against Kilmarnock at Rugby Park, when we started with a midfield of Sullivan, Strachan and Jarvie and lost the game 1-0, I realised I would need to decide finally where to play Strachan. Up to this time we had really been accommodating Gordon. He was a talented player, had a marvellous temperament, wanted to play and was prepared to be on the ball all the time. But I became sure we were really wasting his talents by playing him in centre midfield, because he played too many short balls from that position. He was also easily nailed by the more physical players. We couldn't expect him to win 50/50 tackles or go up against men like Roy Aitken or Tom Forsyth and expect to win the ball off them. I decided to play him on the right side and meanwhile look around the club for a centre midfield player to balance the team.

We always felt that John McMaster should have been a centre midfield player. In his first season with me John lacked consistency although his talent was obvious. As time went on, though, he gained the consistency and became a great player, and, but for injuries, who knows what would have happened? Anyway at that time we were using John on the left midfield where he was vying for position with

Gordon Strachan

Drew Jarvie, so we still needed to find a player within the club who could balance out the likes of John and Gordon or Drew and Gordon. We decided to take Alex McLeish out of the centre-half position and play him in the midfield. We knew Alex was an honest, hard-working boy, desperate to do well. He was destined to become a centre-half but we wanted to give him wider experience. As we later did in the case of Neale Cooper, we made him a centre midfield player for the early part of his career. It worked well for us and made a tremendous difference to the team. A midfield of Strachan, McLeish and Jarvie, or Strachan, McLeish and McMaster had balance, it had toughness and it had quality.

We then saw Gordon Strachan flourish and become the great player of later years. It was as if he had sprouted wings. Obviously he wanted to play for me and that was important. I had brought him into the side the previous season and he became more or less a regular. But when he was out of the team I remember the chairman asked me if I wanted to let him go and I said, 'No, let's just wait.' I had admired him as a player at Dundee. I always admire players with ability, good control, good vision, a sort of cheeky arrogance. People always ask what Gordon's strongest asset is and I always say it is his first touch of the ball. No matter which angle the ball comes at him or at whatever pace, Gordon Strachan will control that ball immediately and that really is his greatest attribute. Another thing that people often overlook is that Gordon Strachan is a good finisher — a high quality finisher. We used to urge him to operate up the park as much as possible because he was always capable of scoring a goal. If you think about it, in his six seasons with me he scored 90 goals. For a midfield player that's not bad going at all.

From the time we made that change the season had been going exceptionally well till we hit that setback against Dundee United in the League Cup Final. But the great thing that we try to develop in people at Pittodrie is how to handle adversity, and how to recover from defeat. I remember coming back up the road from Dens Park that night and really feeling worse than I have felt in my life. It was a strange feeling. We have a funny saying at Aberdeen that when we have a bad result we are heading for the harbour and believe me I really felt that way. I lay awake in bed all night expecting the phone to ring for some reason. I couldn't sleep a wink. In the morning I just felt like packing everything in because the season had promised so much and then we had been beaten by United and lost our first chance of a trophy that year. It was, however, a matter of gathering yourself together, not giving in. As I say to all the young players, if you give in once you give in twice. I gathered myself, got dressed and went into Pittodrie very early. I got myself stripped and met every player coming in the door to congratulate him on his effort in the replay. I stressed it was a time to go on, it was a time to look forward. And I think that period was part of making us what we are today. If you check the records, Aberdeen very seldom lose two in a row.

The rain continued for the rest of that week after the League Cup Final and prior to our game with St Mirren at home. Saturday was a dirty, wet day and I half suggested to the chairman that it would not be a bad idea if this game was postponed because the crowd would be low, the support would be a wee bit disillusioned by losing the way we did, and the players were a bit down. The chairman said, 'Listen, son, get on with the game. You don't quit.' And he was right.

We got on with the game and we beat St Mirren for the first time while I was manager — a good result for us, for they had been a little bit of a thorn in the flesh, gaining unexpected draws. In front of only 5,000 spectators Alex McLeish and Derek Hamilton scored the goals that set us on the way again.

The next week we came up against our bogey team again and this time Morton beat us 1-0 with another late goal at Greenock. We followed that by beating Rangers 3-2 at Pittodrie when Hamilton scored the winner near the end. But I could feel a change in the place. There was a sense of direction about us, as if we knew we were getting there.

By March 1980 the weather had played havoc with our League programme and we were lagging nine points behind Celtic, though with five games in hand. But Celtic's points were in the bag, ours were still to be played for. Celtic had to be favourites. On 22 March, although Pittodrie was covered with snow, ours was the only Premier League match likely to be on and our opponents were — Morton! We made a big effort to stage the game. It was too good an opportunity to miss — if we could get two points here we would be two points nearer Celtic. We still believed we could win the League. In the morning all the pensioners who do so much on the ground at Pittodrie were joined by the kids, the staff and Pat Stanton and myself. We worked like slaves to get that game on. We did, and we won through a Drew Jarvie goal after Mark McGhee, who came on as substitute just after half-time, had torn the Morton defence apart.

That was the start of a run which saw us go fifteen League games without defeat, dropping only four points on the way through draws with Hibs at home, Partick away, Rangers at Ibrox, and Dundee United away. As the momentum gathered with each good result, the sense of occasion grew in the club and among the players. The measure of a team is when it is put into a situation where it can't afford mistakes and everyone has to play well. We had two, maybe three, occasions in that run where that particular belief had to be proved.

One particularly testing period was the week we had to play against Kilmarnock on a Tuesday night at Rugby Park and follow that up with a visit to Celtic Park on the Saturday. The game against Kilmarnock was probably one of the best performances by an Aberdeen team in my years there. You could have set it to music. It was an exhilarating, exciting, football-packed performance. It really was breathtaking, even more than the 4-0 scoreline in our favour suggested. A few English managers who had been at the game weighing up players telephoned me later to say it was the most complete performance from a team they had seen in years. It was especially good to hear that kind of praise coming from English managers who often tend to underrate Scottish football.

For the Saturday match at Parkhead I brought back Drew Jarvie, whom I had rested for the Kilmarnock game despite his great goal-scoring run. We knew we had a great record at Parkhead and we simply knew we were going to win — maybe the same type of feeling Morton used to have when they played us!

40,000 people turned up for the match on a hot, sunny day. At Parkhead the stand shades part of the park so I told the players to make sure they did their warm-up in the shade: 'Don't be going out in that sun and killing yourself.' Now, big Doug Rougvie loved to play at Parkhead and always did his warm-up in front of the Celtic fans in 'The Jungle' on the far side. He simply loved to intimidate them in a jocular way. When I went out to see how the players were getting on with their warm-up, there was Big Doug performing his special act. In baking hot conditions too! I could have killed him. As it was, we won the game 2-1 with goals from Drew Jarvie and Mark McGhee. Bobby Clark saved a Bobby Lennox penalty and that was decisive. We were on a charge and felt nothing could stop us now.

We next beat Dundee at home on a Wednesday night game when Jarvie scored again. Bobby Clark made one of his best-ever saves that night from a young boy, Ferguson, when the score was 1-1. I turned round to Pat Stanton and said, 'That save will win us the League.' Straight after that we went right up the park and scored the winner. Things were going our way. The crowds were starting to come too, sensing the League was within our reach after our victory at Parkhead.

Then came a short break from League football. On 12 April we played a Scottish Cup semi-final against Rangers at Parkhead and despite totally dominating the game we lost to a Derek Johnstone goal with only three or four minutes of the game to go. They had seven players booked. The irony was that we had already played Rangers six times that year, when we won five and drew one. Six victories in one season against Rangers would have been some kind of record.

Following that we dropped a point in a 1-1 draw with Hibs. George Best was playing for them and his presence swelled the Pittodrie crowd to over 17,000 but he did nothing in the match. We were shocking. In fact it was embarrassing. We scored our equaliser about seven minutes into injury time. I remember blowing my top in the dressing room. 'That's us thrown the League away,' I said. 'We were beaten in the semi-final on Saturday when we threw it away, and now we're throwing the League away tonight by drawing with Hibs at home.'

We were still three points behind Celtic with six games to go and with a game in hand over them. On 19 April we went down to Kilmarnock again and won 3-1. But that result was less important than what was happening elsewhere in the country because that day Dundee thrashed Celtic 5-1. We were coming out of the dressing room at half-time, 3-1 up and coasting, when Mr Anderson, the Aberdeen vice-chairman, came along to tell us that Dundee were leading Celtic 3-1. All the players knew, and the second-half of that game was the first time that nerves showed in their play. But it was a good idea to get the nerves out of the road then, for our next match was to be the biggest test yet — Celtic again, at Parkhead.

The atmosphere was fantastic. Celtic Park was a cauldron. The gate was 48,000 but it seemed like 70,000, as if the ground attendance record had been broken. You couldn't move and it was a hot night. I remember my team talk very well. If we were to win the League we wanted to do it the right way and that was to go to Parkhead in a positive mood, to attack them. Nothing else would be good enough. We didn't want to win the League by default, through the efforts of other teams like Dundee who had beaten Celtic 5-1. We wanted to beat Celtic on their own ground, in front of their own people. It was so important to me personally and so important to the players too because at the end of the day the stature they would gain by winning the way they wanted to at Celtic Park would be immense. If they'd done it once, they could do it twice. A famous maxim.

Before the game there was a quietness about the team — something I like to see in the Pittodrie dressing room. I usually have my team talks with the players about an hour-and-a-half before the game. I then disappear from the dressing room, only looking in from

39

time to time. I let the players get on with their own preparations in their own personal way. They've got their own mental build-up and their own physical build-up.

But, as had happened before when we had played Celtic in big games, the kick-off was delayed. Now whether this is 'intentional or not I'm not sure, but at times it seemed to me that they thought perhaps we'd be a bit unnerved by the whole occasion. This time the players were ready for it — they'd experienced it a couple of weeks before in the 2-1 game at Celtic Park and they expected it now. In fact, I remember to this day how Stuart Kennedy handled it absolutely brilliantly. A great character was Stuart. He lay there on the plinth with no boots on, waiting for the late Desmond White to come in and say, 'I'm sorry, lads, but the game will need to be delayed. The police have instructed us there are crowds outside' . . . etc, etc. Stuart was lying there on the plinth with his boots off and just his briefs on. That's all. He had no strip on, no pants, no socks. But as soon as Desmond was out the door he was away getting ready. This was typical of the atmosphere about the place. We were totally prepared for whatever was going to happen that night. The rest, of course, is history but it is worth recording.

We started the game well and attacked Celtic. We proved we were there not just to make up numbers but to win the League. We got the first goal. A Gordon Strachan corner kick was knocked down at the front post. Ian Scanlon had a shot but it was blocked and the ball broke to Steve Archibald who toe-poked it home. Archibald's attitude in scoring that day was important. He went went right across to 'The Jungle' and clenched his fists at them. Now, I don't like to see provocative actions by the players but on that occasion it maybe was a good thing. It was letting Celtic know that we were there to win.

Celtic got back in the game with a very doubtful penalty. Over the years I've been with the club, Aberdeen have become used to penalties being given against them at Celtic Park. They had another penalty claim minutes after that which was more justifiable than the first but it was turned down. The referee had obviously given them their favours and that was the end of it. We were awarded a penalty ourselves just before half-time. John McMaster was brought down by Danny McGrain in a silly tackle on the edge of the box, when he was going away from goal too. Nonetheless it was technically a penalty.

Gordon Strachan missed it. I remember I watched it time and time again on the video and the Celtic's supporters' reaction to Peter Latchford saving that penalty of Gordon's was as if they'd won the Cup or the League itself. It was unbelievable. There was a crescendo of noise. But we weren't to be denied. Right on the stroke of half-time we scored the second goal from a delightful little move involving three or four players. The ball had been knocked out for a corner kick. Andy Watson got it and struck it to Stuart Kennedy. He played it to Gordon Strachan who returned it. Stuart placed a nice cross on Mark McGhee's head and in it went — right on the stroke of half-time. 2-1.

The referee was put under a bit of pressure in the tunnel at half-time. He was obviously a bit nervous about the whole event. It was a big occasion for him. I said, 'Look, you don't need to worry about that. You're here to do your job and referee honestly and fairly. There are two teams who want to win the League out there tonight, not just Celtic. We are here to win it too.' I never go near referees at all now since I got into trouble but on that occasion I felt I had to — there was a League at stake.

Gordon Strachan scored early in the second-half, when Peter Latchford dropped a cross from Ian Scanlon. We were 3-1 up and thereafter there was no danger that we were losing that game. Incidentally, around this time Celtic and ourselves were also vying for the signature of Frank McGarvey. Of course he was a Celtic supporter and obviously made Celtic his first choice. But we were disappointed and felt a little bit let down that he had agreed to come to us and then Celtic had come in at the last minute. These things happen. If he didn't want to come, that was fine. But I remember the next day the *Daily Record* had a heading on the back page, alongside photographs of me in red and Billy McNeill in green. It read, 'McNeill the Winner.' I went into the players and said, 'Aye, he might win this one but he'll not win the war.' 'By the way, I'm no bloody loser either.' It gave everyone a wee bit more determination. In the end it just fired us up a wee bit more. You need causes sometimes for motivation and there is no doubt we used that cause and causes like that from time to time. You remind yourself of the number of people who don't want you to win. It fires you up, it gets you going, so we use it to our own advantage.

We got over the Celtic game and the run-in after that was euphoric. We beat St Mirren 2-0 at home on a smashing day in front of 19,000 or 20,000 people. I remember wee Gordon was troubled with constipation and stomach trouble, but he played that day and did well to get through the match. Then we went down to Tannadice on the Wednesday and Gordon Strachan scored a great goal from a 25-yard free kick. United came back at us in the second-half and we drew 1-1. The next match was, of course, the day we won the League — 3 May 1980.

We hadn't a particularly good record at Easter Road. Most matches down there had ended in draws. Celtic were playing at Love Street that day and while we were sitting at Easter Road watching the game we were wondering what was happening at the other side of the country. Of course the press at Easter Road are quite near to the directors' box so we were getting up-to-the-minute information from various sources. It was still 0-0 in our match and we'd started getting quite confident. After 15 or 16 minutes I couldn't see Hibs scoring. They, of course, were already relegated. Then the breaking point came. We were given a free kick on the right. It was worked by John McMaster and Gordon Strachan and I think it was McMaster that played it in. Steve Archibald got in ahead of George Stewart, the Hibs centre-half who was a big rugged customer. I had said to Steve before the game, 'If George Stewart's on the park, you can bet your life they will be trying like bears because he is a winner.' But Steve nipped in in front of him for that free kick, put us ahead and a minute later we sewed it up. Doug Rougvie took a throw in, Mark McGhee touched it on, beat a defender and then rolled it across the edge of the six-yard box. Andy Watson came in late and scored the second goal. The second-half was a celebration really. Aberdeen supporters had made their minds up we'd won the League. We scored three further goals through Ian Scanlon, who got two, and Mark McGhee.

A great occasion, a great performance. But we still didn't know if we'd won the League. Celtic were still 0-0 and their game was going on later than ours. I went down to the track at time-up and said to Jarvie and Bell, who were the subs, 'It's still 0-0.' The players thought we'd won the League. The crowd were going bananas anyway, cheering and dancing and singing. The champagne corks were popping. It was just a big party. We had a great support down that day, a marvellous turnout. They could sense that we were on the verge of winning the Championship. They knew that we were only a kick of the ball away from it and they were there to see it happening for the first time for many years, since 1954-55. They were there to celebrate.

Eventually I looked up to the press box and Alastair Guthrie, who writes for the *Aberdeen Evening Express*, was there. He put the hand signals, 0-0, up. The rest of it I forget, but I sprinted on that park hugging everybody that got in my road. I felt particularly pleased for players like Bobby Clark because it was the one thing he hadn't won. He won a League Cup Badge when Ally McLeod was manager, he got the Scottish Cup Badge under Eddie Turnbull and this honour was now to be added to his collection — the Premier Division Championship. To be the first provincial team outside the Old Firm to win the League for fifteen years was a tremendous achievement. It was a great day. I

The players with the Championship Trophy

was pleased for all the players really, but more so for Willie Miller, the captain, and Bobby Clark, because these players had been at the club a while.

So we won the League. The end to a marvellous season. It gave us the smell of success. It whetted our appetite. The more success you achieve the hungrier you get. As far as I am concerned, that pursuit of success is now part of my life.

Reflecting on that season, I remember all the help I received from Pat Stanton, then my assistant manager. I had brought Pat into the Aberdeen set-up when I joined the club. He was the kind of person I admired — an honest man with a dry sense of humour, a very witty person with a good knowledge of the game. He was a quiet, unassuming type and our different personalities balanced well. It it was a partnership I was genuinely sorry to see break up at the end of that season when he wanted to go on his own.

Pat had been a great player with Hibs and latterly Celtic. His background was perfect for me and I had already got on well with him at coaching schools in Largs and in the couple of times I played in Scottish League teams with him. At Aberdeen we had a marvellous relationship and I felt I could trust him with my life. It saddened me the way it all turned sour for him at his great love, Hibs, and all the problems he encountered there obviously hurt him deeply. Although people say that the most important relationship in a football club is between manager and assistant manager, they are wrong. It's between the manager and the chairman, as Pat was to find out at Easter Road a few years later.

Another person who'd been supportive to me that season was my brother Martin, whom I was using to do some scouting for the club. After the title-clinching game at Easter Road I saw him after I'd done the press interviews. Our first response was simply to hug each other, I suppose as a way of saying to each other what a pity it was that our father wasn't there to share the celebration.

And what a night of celebration it was! Martin had his car but said, 'Bugger it, I'm coming to Aberdeen with you!' Then wee Gordon Strachan, who had arranged to stay down in Edinburgh with his parents for the Saturday night, offered to take Martin's car and bring it to Dundee on the Sunday, where the team were due to play in a testimonial match for Jocky Scott. Martin said that would be fine and asked Gordon to phone his wife to tell her that he had gone to Aberdeen. Typically, Gordon phoned up Martin's wife, Sandra: 'Mrs Ferguson? This is Gordon Strachan. Martin asked me to phone and tell you he's away to Aberdeen and I've taken his car.' No sooner had Sandra blurted out, 'He's what?', than the bold Gordon banged the phone down. The wee man didn't want any confrontations with anybody. He simply passed the message on and that was the end of it!

So Martin came up to Aberdeen with us. We had a great party on the bus, stopping for extra champagne at a hotel in Kinross where we bought up all the available bubbly — some six bottles. It was the first time I saw Stuart Kennedy ever drink. Stuart is a teetotaller, non-drinker, non-smoker, a fitness fanatic. For the first time in his life, he had a drink.

I remember hearing some of the stories after that night when they all arrived in Mr G's restaurant in Aberdeen and some of the reserve players and the first-team players' wives were there waiting. There was a big party, as you can imagine. When Kennedy came in Willie Garner was there and he thought Stuart was acting it because he never expected to see him with a drink in him. But Stuart was by that time well and truly flying. Apparently he was in great fettle and had the red and white tammy and scarf on the whole night.

Later that night too I was taken up on an invitation. Bill Barclay, the folk singer and comedian who appears on Radio Forth and does the tannoy for Hibs, had asked me to come out and see the support after the match. We were all on the park and the supporters were chanting my name. I went into the commentary box and spoke to them over the mike and I thanked them all for their support. I told them I loved them all and said anybody who would like to come to the house tonight, could come. So, half-way through the night, about 3 o'clock in the morning, the bell goes at the house and here are two supporters: 'Can we come in for a drink?' I said, 'Certainly you can, in you come.' I introduced my brother. My wife had gone to bed by that time. We'd played the video over about three or four times, but we played it back to show the two supporters. I don't know to this day who they were. They introduced themselves certainly, but that just completed the night. As I say, celebrate your victories and mourn your defeats.

That was the end of the season and it was also the end of Steve Archibald's time at Aberdeen. Steve played against Partick on the Wednesday night and that was his last game. We had agreed that Steve was desperate to get away and with freedom of contract coming up we didn't want to stand in his way. We knew we could get good money. We had told the player that we would let him go at the end of the season if we got a good enough offer, and we transferred him to Tottenham Hotspur.

But Steve was a great player for me. For two years I was manager when Steve was at the club. The first of those was an up and down season for him. But there was no doubt about his keenness and ambition to improve and the energy he spent on trying to do just that. In that second year I had to take my hat off to him because he worked like a beast. Around that time when we introduced zone play — a system where defenders, midfielders and attackers have to operate in their own specific areas of the park — Steve really became effective. It was like a revelation and must have been so for him too. Previously with Clyde, he had acted as a midfielder and sometimes even played at centre-half or full-back. I remember when I was at St Mirren I had a scout watch Steve playing right-back with Clyde and his report was, to say the least, average! With Aberdeen, Steve became a first-class international striker.

I would say, up to the time that Gordon Strachan left, that he was one of the few players I would have taken back to Aberdeen. A lot of players have come and gone over the years but there is no doubt about it, Steve Archibald and Gordon Strachan were two I would have taken back in a minute. Because of freedom of contract nowadays you are not always going to hold on to your best players and you're not going to hold on to them all anyway, but those two I would have taken back any time.

Steve is his own man. Many people don't seem to like him but I think he got bad reports from some quarters simply because of the fact that he didn't have any time for the press. He is a private person in many ways, a great family man. The stories about him always being in my office were true. He would be in there every day. We used to call where he sat, 'The Archibald Chair', and I remember when he came back up with Tottenham after they had won the FA Cup to play in Willie Miller's testimonial, we had the chair all decorated with an 'Archibald's Chair' label on and invited him in. He couldn't see the funny side of it. 'We've always called it Archibald's Chair,' I said. He said, 'You don't have a sign on it?' I said, 'Yes we do, of course we do.' He wouldn't believe it. It was a great laugh.

I liked him. As a player, I found him an aggressive, quick, resilient type, rarely injured. He had two good feet, was good in the air and seemed to have a spring about him. He was like Denis Law in terms of a shot coming off a goalkeeper — Archibald was always first in. Alive to situations, a good touch on the ball. I told Keith Burkinshaw that for Steve to really develop the one thing he had to do is turn on men. He didn't turn enough on men and attack them. He always wanted to lay balls off, with his back to the game, instead of maybe doing more positive things himself or attempting a more individual approach in terms of turning on opponents and running at them. He is capable of doing this and he could have developed that way if he'd stayed at Aberdeen, I'm sure of it.

But I had no complaints about him as a player. I had some blazing rows with him but at the end of the day you knew he would play on a Saturday and I admire that in anyone. Also he had the courage to state his case, say what he wanted out of life. There was no doubt that Steve had ambition to do well and I know he'll succeed. Whatever he does he'll always do well because he's hungry and he'll achieve what he wants to achieve. It was sad when he left because I felt if we could have kept Steve we could have gone on to really good things. We were going into the European Cup and I wanted him to stay but it was his way and it was good money for both him and us.

I met Keith Burkinshaw and one of the Spurs directors, a Mr Richardson, down in Edinburgh and we agreed a deal. The chairman and I went to London to complete it. At the time Ardiles had come back from injury and the Argentine national side were about to play England at Wembley. After we concluded the Archibald deal we watched Argentina train at White Hart Lane and there I saw a young player with awesome shooting ability. All he did was practise shooting. He was bending shots and generally turning on an incredible

Raising the Championship Flag, the first time since 1954-55

performance and Ardiles sat and spoke to us about him. He said, 'This is going to be one of the greatest players in the world.' His name was Diego Maradona. And although it hasn't actually been proven that he is the world's greatest — his temperament and ability to handle adversity are both suspect — nonetheless, it was a treat to sit there and watch that display of shooting and also to chat to someone as pleasant and likeable as Ardiles who told us about Argentinian training methods.

Reflecting on that year and thinking particularly of the striker's role, it's also interesting to consider if we would still have won the League if we'd had Joe Harper fit to play for the rest of the season. Everyone had their own opinions about Joe. I thought he was a marvellous player but he never fulfilled his potential because basically he wasn't a hard trainer. I never knew him to complete a pre-season programme. Nevertheless he was a magnificent finisher and had an excellent football brain. Joe was the hero of the Aberdeen Beach End for many a year and is still something of a legend in the North-East.

Personally, I don't think we would have won the League Championship with Joe in the side. He was a bit of a luxury at times, and away from home in particular. He wasn't the hardest worker and always had a bit of a weight problem and we knew from the start of that season that the system we were playing would require a higher workrate from the strikers. Steve Archibald was a natural hard worker but I felt at the time that Steve was possibly doing more of Joe's work than Joe himself. If he was more or less guaranteeing you a goal a game then you would go along with it. We were always looking for Joe to score but away from home (and that's where we won the League that season — away from home) he was less effective. I always think that if Joe had been younger when I arrived at Pittodrie, I could have done something with him, but then again other managers could probably have said that too.

Harper's injury at Parkhead opened the door for Mark McGhee. We had bought Mark the previous Easter, just a few days before we played Rangers in the League Cup Final. If I had had him a week longer he would have played in that Final but as it was he wasn't ready. In fact he played his first game for Aberdeen in a reserve match at Ibrox the night before and scored a goal.

Mark took a long time to settle in with Aberdeen and in fact many thought he might turn out to be a waste of money. But I had great belief in him. I had actually tried to sign him when I was manager at St Mirren in a swop deal for a St Mirren player called Donny McDowall but Morton, his club at that time, wanted £5,000 more than we could

Mark McGhee

afford and the deal slipped by. Lo and behold, two years later I had the chance to buy him — from Newcastle for £70,000, and it turned out to be one of the best bits of business we ever did.

He was a strong, resilient character, Mark, and hard to knock off the ball, but at that early part of his time with Aberdeen he was inconsistent. When he came on at Parkhead as substitute for Harper and scored a goal, it was something of a turning point but we still obviously had to have someone else to push him, to give us extra cover among the strikers. We tried Drew Jarvie up there and we had a young lad, Derek Hamilton, who came as a full-back but showed promise as a

49

good finisher. Hamilton was quick and had two good feet so we tried him. But we never quite got the continuous partnership. Striking partnerships should grow with continuity of playing alongside each other such that a kind of telepathy develops between the partners. That is one thing that began to happen that season: Archibald and McGhee began to develop an understanding.

But that was the end of an era, the end of Harper's time at Aberdeen and the end of Archibald's time. There was also, though, a great feeling of optimism and togetherness among those involved in the club. In winning the League for the first time since 1955 the players had responded magnificently. I felt that to a man they were united in their loyalty to me as manager and that is as important an aspect as any other in the player-manager relationship. It was obvious that I had won them over and equally obvious that they had won me over. One particular incident demonstrated this fact.

I was in a deep sleep one Sunday morning at 2 am when the phone rang. When I picked it up a chorus of singing came from the other end. The lads were having a celebration party over at Willie Miller's house and decided that I deserved a rendition of one of their musical pieces. When I blurted out that they were all fined and suspended for irresponsible behaviour I was met with another chorus — of derision.

After I hung up I lay back and reflected how satisfied I was that my relationship with the players was close enough for them to have reacted like that. But on Monday I exacted my revenge by taking them up one of our regular pre-season hill runs at Seaton Park. I informed them that we were about to have a thirty-minute hill run for the benefit of the Mike Samme Singers and off they went. When they returned, though, Alex McLeish was complaining bitterly that 'Mike Samme' himself had escaped the punishment. He was obviously referring to Willie Miller who had wisely reported an injury and didn't train that day.

We were into the summer and the irony was that although we'd won the League, we weren't well enough known at the time to be invited to lucrative summer tours abroad — that was exclusive to the Celtics and the Rangers and the Arsenals and the Manchester Uniteds, Liverpools and Tottenhams. We therefore fell back on an invitation from an Aberdeen lad, Dave Graham, who was running a team up in the Faroe Islands. He kept phoning us for a game, so, when he quoted reasonable money for us to go up there, we decided it was on.

I remember the Faroes as a barren place but the real fishing folk made it quite an occasion. We had a great time but the landing and take off through those mountains was terrible. The pilot's name was

Plunkett. After the match we let the players out for a night as the season was finished. Plunkett was spotted having more than a few beers and I can tell you there was more than a little consternation among our group about the next morning's early take-off!

Going across in the ferry to the stadium it looked just like the end of the world. One of the players, Kennedy or Strachan, said: 'Can you imagine what would have happened if we'd lost the League, if this is the reward for winning it?'

On the coach with the trophy

PREMIER DIVISION CHAMPIONSHIP

	P	W	L	D	F	A	Pts
ABERDEEN	36	19	7	10	68	36	48
CELTIC	36	18	7	11	61	38	47
ST MIRREN	36	15	9	12	56	49	42
DUNDEE UNITED	36	12	11	13	43	30	37
RANGERS	36	15	14	7	50	46	37
MORTON	36	14	14	8	51	46	36
PARTICK THISTLE	36	11	11	14	43	47	36
KILMARNOCK	36	11	14	11	36	52	33
DUNDEE	36	10	20	6	47	73	26
HIBERNIAN	36	6	24	6	29	67	18

SCOTTISH CUP

Third Round	Arbroath	Away	D	1-1	
Replay	Arbroath	Home	W	5-0	
Fourth Round	Airdrie	Home	W	8-0	
Fifth Round	Partick Thistle	Away	W	2-1	
Semi-final	Rangers	Parkhead	L	0-1	

LEAGUE CUP

1st R 1st leg	Arbroath	Home	W	4-0	
2nd leg	Arbroath	Away	L	1-2	
2nd R 1st leg	Meadowbank	Away	W	5-0	
2nd leg	Meadowbank	Home	D	2-2	
3rd R 1st leg	Rangers	Home	W	3-1	
2nd leg	Rangers	Away	W	2-0	
Q-final 1st leg	Celtic	Home	W	3-2	
2nd leg	Celtic	Away	W	1-0	
Semi-final	Morton	Hampden	W	2-1	
Final	Dundee United	Hampden	D	0-0	AET
Replay	Dundee United	Dens	L	0-3	

UEFA CUP

1st R 1st leg	Eintracht Frankfurt	Home	D	1-1	
2nd leg	Eintracht Frankfurt	Away	L	0-1	1-2

Top Scorer: Steve Archibald 21

Chapter Three
1980-81: Learning from Liverpool

HAVING NOW won my first trophy with Aberdeen — the Premier League Championship of 1979-80 — I couldn't wait for the next season to begin. I was learning something about myself — my hunger and restlessness for more success. I took the family for a holiday to Majorca that summer to recharge my batteries. I also took my training programmes and, as always, spent many an hour planning out new ideas. I was desperate for the start of the season and full of enthusiasm and self-belief. Psychologically, that League win helped me to realise that my job as manager at Aberdeen was safe and that I could use the success to build a better future for the club. The players had begun to really respond to me and I felt I now had a real grasp of my role as manager.

Domestically, too, everything was more content. Cathy, my wife, was beginning to appreciate the quality of life in Aberdeen. We had settled in well in our house and the kids were enjoying school.

It goes without saying that without the total support of your wife and family it is impossible to get on with your job of managing footballers. So it is the case in our family. Cathy has sacrificed a normal husband-wife relationship for my career as firstly a player and now a manager and it is a painful admission on my part to say that the rearing of our three sons has been left to her, particularly when they were young and I had two public houses in Glasgow at the same time as I was manager of St Mirren. I very rarely saw them during the week, and only at weekends did I manage to resume the role of father. I remember on Christmas Day 1976 St Mirren played Clydebank in a top of the League clash which had caught the imagination of the public. The game finished 2-2 but there was an incident in the second-half when the linesman gave offside against us and I reacted badly and chased up the touchline after him, only to be pulled back by Clydebank manager Bill Munro. My reaction had been unnecessary but at the time I was under a lot of personal strain. I had even had to personally prepare Christmas dinners at one of my pubs three nights in a row as my cook had quit. That night I picked Cathy and the boys up at her mother's. She noticed how tired I was and immediately on arriving home put the kids to bed and told me to have a sleep on the chair while she prepared something to eat. I lay on that chair and I swear I could hear every word on the TV though Cathy maintains I snored right through. But there is one example of the sacrifice she and the family have made. No family Christmas dinner and an early night for her and the kids.

With so many good omens it was ironic that season 1980-81 turned out to be one of only limited success for the club. Never in my time as manager has one club been so badly hit at such inconvenient times by injury to key players. I must admit the season was a nightmare from the start. First of all Bobby Clark came back from the summer break and reported a severe back. problem due largely, I still believe, to excessive weight training. So, right at the beginning of the season I was faced with the prospect of relying heavily on a relatively inexperienced 20-year-old goalkeeper — Jim Leighton. Although I was already convinced that Jim would be a great player, I told the directors that I wanted to look for an experienced goalkeeper.

At the start of the season we played against Twente Enschede, a Dutch team, in a friendly match at Pittodrie. They had one or two very useful players — Zondervan among them — and when I had dinner with their manager after the match I asked if he would consider selling us his goalkeeper. He naturally refused but told me in all seriousness that he had another keeper on his club's books — a Belgian — who was very good indeed and whom he would let me have for a small fee. I thought it was a bit of a gamble but he insisted: 'The goalkeepers in continental Europe are excellent. If you need a goalkeeper it's the place you must look.' My experience certainly led me to agree. I don't know how many times I've gone on pre-season tours in Germany and Holland and played amateur teams whose goalkeepers have been brilliant. I took a chance and signed Marc de Clerck.

In many ways that signing proved to be one of the best deals I've ever made, although he only played a few competitive games for us. One game he did play was at Berwick in a League Cup tie and this was the source of a difficult quiz question some time later: 'Which Belgian footballer was transferred from a Dutch team to a Scottish team and scored in his debut on English soil?' And of course it was Marc de Clerck in Berwick. But Marc, too, fell prone to our injury jinx that season and sustained a knee injury when his studs caught in the turf on his League debut against Kilmarnock. So, although we had signed Marc to give Jim Leighton time to develop, Jim found himself having to develop faster than we had anticipated. He responded magnificently and was given every help and encouragement from the big Belgian.

It was marvellous to have Marc about the place, for his sheer professionalism and his attitude to training brought something to the club. He was continually developing training ideas for Jim Leighton and making sure he performed them, even when it became clear that he couldn't win his own place back in the team because Jim was doing so well. Marc was a great character and a real personality and is still a friend of Aberdeen. In fact he and his wife later joined us when we played Waterschei in the semi-final of the European Cup-Winners' Cup and also came to the final in Gothenburg.

I knew within probably a couple of weeks of that season that we were going to miss Archibald and that that was probably going to be the biggest problem of all. I reckon we missed him so much in season 1980-81 that we just never recovered. We tried playing Jarvie just behind one striker, Mark McGhee, with Ian Scanlon at outside-left. That's how we played our opening game and although that formation could be considered successful I was convinced we were not as potent up front as we had been.

That whole season I looked for replacements for Steve. I tried Yugoslavs, a coloured lad from Luton Town, a Danish striker. I signed Andy Harrow and Walker McCall and travelled over to watch yet another Danish striker. But you just can't replace people like Steve Archibald easily and I learned a lesson from that — replace before you sell if you know a player is going to leave. Later, when it became obvious that we couldn't hold on to Gordon Strachan, we were able to replace him with Billy Stark a year before. Billy came to Pittodrie knowing that Gordon was leaving.

Despite these problems, though, we had made a good start to the season. Although we went out of the League Cup to Dundee we had won the Drybrough Cup, beating St Mirren in the Final. In the League we strung together fifteen matches without defeat and if you added those to our last fifteen matches of the season before that, it was thirty League games in a row without a defeat — surely a record of some sort! Inevitably we lost our sixteenth League match that season to 'you know who' at Cappielow. After that we reached the New Year period without further League defeat before everything finally collapsed.

The real lessons of that year were learned in European competition. In the first round of the European Cup we were drawn against Austria Memphis, whom we defeated 1-0 at Pittodrie in the first leg. Over in Austria I told the players I thought we could do well if

55

we kept our heads and learned to keep possession of the ball, especially as it was a big pitch. McLeish was injured so I played Willie Garner. As it was they played without strikers and played too wide. We put up a great tactical performance with better possession of the ball than in previous European matches and drew 0-0 to go through to the next round.

When we drew Liverpool for that next round there was an excitement and euphoria throughout the Aberdeen area in particular but the match also caught the imagination of the whole of Scotland. Some people still say that the best thing that happened to Aberdeen was meeting Liverpool in the European Cup that season and while I can see some truth in that in the long term, in the short term it was nothing less than a nightmare.

The prospect of our matches with Liverpool dominated and interrupted everything. Through lack of concentration we started to struggle a bit in our League matches, putting in inferior performances. We played Dundee in the League Cup just prior to meeting Liverpool and our performance was shoddy and totally lacking in quality, hunger or drive. It was as if the shadow of Anfield had engulfed Dens Park. We drew 0-0, then lost in the return leg at home to a late Cammy Fraser goal. Almost as bad as the result was that we also lost Stuart Kennedy with an injury in the early part of the game and that was certainly unsettling. Even so, on reflection, I still don't believe for a minute that we would have lost to Dundee if the Liverpool tie hadn't been looming. We never really got to grips with the whole prospect. It got to us. It got to everyone.

Archie Knox and I went down to Anfield to see Liverpool playing Middlesbrough. By that time Liverpool had gone something like 76 home games without defeat, conceding only some twenty-odd goals in these matches — an unbelievable record. It was obvious they were a team with an abundance of experience and genuine skill — Clemence, Neal, Ray Kennedy, Alan Kennedy, Hansen, Thompson, Souness, Dalglish. No one doubted it would be a difficult task to get any kind of decent result out of our games.

I decided to play the same system as Liverpool, 4-4-2, for our first leg at Pittodrie, with Jarvie trying to keep Souness busy and also getting into the box to support the front two of Scanlon and McGhee. Like all the best laid plans that one went astray in the first five minutes of the match. John McMaster was going across the park with the ball when Ray Kennedy went over the top in a tackle and caught him badly below the knee. McMaster went down and while he was still on the ground they broke away and scored a clever goal with McDermott chipping Jim Leighton from almost the bye-line.

From then on it was all uphill and although we battled gamely and some moves almost paid off, they kept the ball well. The Liverpool players had a bit of grit and nastiness about them, good qualities when you need them, and handled the whole game well. They were also well armed in the psychological warfare stakes. As the players came in for half-time they used those psychology tactics to the full. That aspect was educative for us and we were later to put such psychology to good use in our European matches, especially in the European Cup-Winners' Cup Final against Real Madrid. Football is a learning process and we learned something that night.

We learned even more from the visit to Anfield. Again the psychology was being played as well as the football. The Anfield crowd itself was an electric experience for our lads. John McMaster was obviously unavailable — after the Pittodrie game he was out of football for a year — and Stuart Kennedy was missing too. With 20-year-old Jim Leighton in goal and young Andy Dornan at left-back, we decided to play two markers, Rougvie and McLeish, against Dalglish and Johnstone, with Willie Miller free and Doug Bell protecting the right-back area against Ray Kennedy who was stronger than Strachan. We played Gordon infield that night.

For most of that first-half we played well, containing them efficiently. While Mark McGhee should have scored for us, they had hardly had a shot at goal. Then, from a corner kick with just seven minutes of the first-half remaining, Willie Miller uncharacteristically sliced the ball past Jim Leighton and into the net. A minute later they scored again. Suddenly it was half-time and we were trailing 2-0 and really up against it.

Here we were 2-0 down at Anfield and 3-0 down over the two legs against a team who had gone 76 home games without defeat. I was lecturing the players on what they were doing wrong and how we could correct it when Drew Jarvie — I love him, for you cannot help but love a man with the optimism he produced that night — piped up, 'Come on, lads, three quick goals and we're back in it.' There was a stunned silence for a minute or two until we grasped the full meaning of his words. Three quick goals against a Liverpool team undefeated at Anfield for almost two years! It was priceless.

The second-half was a procession. They demonstrated possession of the ball, delicate passes and deft touch control. All the qualities that great sides had, Liverpool had that night. Towards the end of the game I told Willie Garner — I was still banned from the bench and Willie was acting as runner for me — that we might as well put on young

Neale Cooper for the experience. 'And,' I said, 'while you're down there, tell the referee to blow the bloody whistle!' That summed up how I felt. I was never so glad to get a game out of the way in my whole life.

In the short term being drawn against Liverpool was bad for us. In anticipation of the matches our form in the League faded and we were knocked out of the League Cup. We tried to recover from the Liverpool games as best we could, to use it as part of a learning process for the players. I told the players that the most important thing was how we recovered from the experience and went on from there.

Immediately we reacted. We went to Parkhead on the Saturday without Kennedy and McMaster and also without Miller, who had in fact played against Liverpool with a slight hamstring problem — one of the reasons we had decided to play him as sweeper. The injuries were certainly beginning to take their toll but, as I said, we don't lose twice in a row too often: we beat Celtic 2-0 with goals from our recent signing, Walker McCall, and a marvellous performance from young Neale Cooper who played centre-back in place of Miller. He was obviously a player of the future.

By the end of 1980 we were five points clear of our rivals in the League. Then fate took over and ruined everything. On 30 December we played Dundee United in front of a full house at Pittodrie. It was a marvellous match and ended fairly in a 1-1 draw, but it was also the game in which Gordon Strachan sustained the injury which put him out for the rest of the season. It was an especially bad blow to us coming on top of the long-term injuries to Bobby Clark and John McMaster. Our midfield was now well and truly scuppered at a vital point of the season. Gordon more than anyone would be missed as a source of inspiration. In fact to this day I believe we would have taken the League title that year if we had been able to play a full strength side and perhaps also if we hadn't played those two games against Liverpool which hurt us both physically and psychologically.

Things really started to slide when we went to Ibrox at the end of January. We had to play that match without Clark, McMaster, Strachan, Willie Miller, who was suspended, and Stuart Kennedy, who had an eye injury. Half the team that had won the League the previous season was missing for that important game. We were forced to play a young team with Ian Angus and Neil Simpson in the middle of the park, Doug Considine at left-back and Derek Hamilton at right-back. With such a weakened team it would have been surprising if we had won and in the end we went down 1-0 to a late Derek Johnstone goal.

We also lost our next game — against bogey team Morton — and that was the one time in the season we lost two games in a row. Next we drew with Airdrie and lost to St Mirren and that was it. In the space of a month we'd lost everything. Celtic passed us in the League and we just never recovered. They won the Championship by seven points.

As I said, season 1980-81 was one in which we had more than our fair share of injuries but as a manager I had to accept the inevitability of that situation. I just had to make the best of what I had and get on with planning for the next game. But although we were a good team and had won the League in 1980, I couldn't help feeling that there was still something missing, that we needed to raise standards for the future.

In fact, in many ways the future was looking quite good. In my first season at Aberdeen I had signed half a dozen young boys. My first was John Hewitt who really came on to score so many important goals, including the famous one in Gothenburg. Then there was Neil Simpson, Ian Angus, Neale Cooper, Eric Black, Bryan Gunn and Steve Cowan, all signed in that one year. It is amazing how those six or seven players have come through to become established Aberdeen players and some of them have even gone on to gain international recognition.

Hewitt celebrates a Rougvie goal

It is a tribute to the coaching at Aberdeen Football Club and a marvellous tribute to the scouting. That was one thing I had going that season — we were able to introduce Neale Cooper in that vital game at Celtic where he played excellently and never gave Frank McGarvey a kick of the ball. We were also able to introduce Neil Simpson, Ian Angus and John Hewitt as the season went on. Although it was a topsyturvy season and we were disappointed at not winning anything, that was a glimmer of hope. Good quality young players were coming through and have continued to do so. Now we have some fine young players at Aberdeen in the same position, all signed at the same time, as sixteen-year-olds. Joe Miller, Paul Wright, Steven Gray, David Robertson, John Lawrence, Robert McRobb — all these young players in time will prove just as good as the players who have now made it.

But back then, in 1981, I also had my eye on another emerging young player, Peter Weir, whom I had signed as a young boy for St Mirren. In fact we made enquiries for Weir the previous summer but St Mirren just weren't interested. I was convinced that Weir with his height, strength, good stamina and two-footed ability would give us quality and width on the left-hand side and improve the team measurably. That summer we managed to come to terms with St Mirren, with Weir coming to us and Ian Scanlon and £220,000 going to them. A lot of people questioned that decision at the time, especially as Scanlon was a popular player with the supporters and in the dressing room. People asked why I didn't keep both but at the end of the day what really swung the deal with St Mirren was the fact that they were receiving a player as well as money. Added to that was the consideration that Ian was now approaching his 30th birthday.

Management is about making the right decisions and I just knew we had to get Peter Weir. With him on the left and Strachan hopefully back on the right side the team had a good balance with quality crosses coming in from both flanks. The uncertainty about John McMaster's future after a bad injury helped me to make the decision. An additional factor was that I felt it important for the supporters to realise that after we had sold Archibald for some £800,000 we were still looking to strengthen the side and were not afraid to spend money. If you sell big, you can also buy big. The Weir signing was good for everyone.

The end of the season also marked Archie Knox's first year with Aberdeen. He had taken a bit of time to settle in as my assistant for he had Dundee United habits when he first came. He eventually realised that the Aberdeen way is different and he became a marvellous asset, working all hours of the day and religiously taking the young players back to the park for extra coaching just about every afternoon. He was

Peter Weir

61

well liked but was also a stickler for discipline. I remember, not too long after Archie started with the club, that he had asked one of the young boys, Alan Lyons, to wash his car. The lad hadn't done it properly so Archie telephoned him at 5 o'clock on the Friday afternoon and told him to get himself back to the park to finish the job off. The boy learned that day — if you're going to do a job, do it right.

Archie, though, also has a good sense of humour. I was sitting at home one Sunday night when Mrs Barker, who ran the digs where three or four of our young players were staying in Summerhill Road, telephoned. 'Enough is enough,' she said. 'I want them all out at the end of the season.' I asked what was wrong. She said, 'They were playing hide-and-seek last night.' I thought, wait a minute, these boys are seventeen-years-old. 'Are you sure?' I asked. 'I'm telling you,' she replied. 'And they've broken a storage heater.'

I telephoned Archie about it and we had a right good laugh. Then we planned our tactics. When they came in in the morning Archie would take them through to the multi-gym, then send each one of them through to me one at a time for questioning. The first three wouldn't say a word about it, but they were a bit more experienced than the last one, 16-year-old Billy Muir, who had just joined the club. I issued the almighty threat: 'You're just here, son, but you'll be going back down the road tomorrow if you don't tell us the truth.' He blurted it out. They *had* been playing hide-and-seek. I then got the four of them together and told them that if they behaved like children, we were going to treat them like children. Everybody had to learn a nursery rhyme for the next day. Archie conducted the session and the star of the show was undoubtedly big Neale Cooper with his moving rendition of *Ba Ba Black Sheep*!

Neale Cooper

PREMIER DIVISION CHAMPIONSHIP

	P	W	L	D	F	A	Pts
CELTIC	36	26	6	4	84	37	56
ABERDEEN	36	19	6	11	61	26	49
RANGERS	36	16	8	12	60	32	44
ST MIRREN	36	18	10	8	56	47	44
DUNDEE UNITED	36	17	10	9	66	42	43
PARTICK THISTLE	36	10	16	10	32	48	30
AIRDRIE	36	10	17	9	36	55	29
MORTON	36	10	18	8	36	58	28
KILMARNOCK	36	5	22	9	23	65	19
HEARTS	36	6	24	6	27	71	18

SCOTTISH CUP

Third Round	Raith Rovers	Away	W	2-1
Fourth Round	Morton	Away	L	0-1

LEAGUE CUP

2nd R 1st leg	Berwick	Home	W	8-1
2nd leg	Berwick	Away	W	4-0
3rd R 1st leg	Rangers	Away	L	0-1
2nd leg	Rangers	Home	W	3-1
Q-final 1st leg	Dundee	Away	D	0-0
2nd leg	Dundee	Home	L	0-1

EUROPEAN CUP

1st R 1st leg	Austria Vienna	Home	W	1-0	
2nd leg	Austria Vienna	Away	D	0-0	1-0
2nd R 1st leg	Liverpool	Home	L	0-1	
2nd leg	Liverpool	Away	L	0-4	0-5

Top Scorer: Mark McGhee 17

Chapter Four
1981-82: A Hampden Triumph

AS NORMAL, much of our pre-season training for season 1981-82 took place up at Gordonstoun, where Archie Knox and I put the players through their paces. We came down from there for a friendly against Dunfermline where Pat Stanton was now manager but that turned out to be an uninspired 1-1 draw. Finally we rounded off our preparations by playing host in a pre-season tournament featuring Aberdeen, Southampton, West Ham and Manchester United — a great boost for our players and supporters alike.

It was a marvellous tournament. We beat West Ham 3-0 in the first game while Southampton accounted for Manchester United. Then we gave Southampton a real roasting in the Final, beating them 5-1 on the Sunday. There were many pleasing aspects to our performances. Peter Weir made a substantial impact on our supporters but so too did Dougie Bell, a player I had taken from St Mirren in a free transfer at the end of my first season with Aberdeen. Bell was a player of tremendous skill, strength and individuality. He played so well in that tournament that we knew it was going to be a great season for him. Eric Black, another young player of great promise, was also introduced to the first team in that competition.

Overall I felt that there was real quality to the players who were coming to play their part in the club and that, together with the Weir signing, encouraged me to look forward to this season with optimism and ambition. We now had a good, solid base to the club and a good working appetite among the players and the staff. The season couldn't come quickly enough.

We had a mixed start in our League Cup fixtures, beating Kilmarnock easily by 3-0 in the first match at Pittodrie, but then losing 1-0 to Hearts down at Tynecastle on a hot, steamy Wednesday night. Peter Weir showed the first after-affects of his transfer that night. When players join Aberdeen from other clubs they often take time to adjust to the different standard of training and fitness. Only one or two — Steve Archibald and Stewart McKimmie immediately come to mind — have been able to adjust relatively easily. The hard pre-season training, the tournament games against West Ham and Southampton and the hard game with Kilmarnock on top of a Wednesday night game were just a little too much for Peter at that time. The rest of the League Cup Section went well for us though and we were drawn to meet Berwick Rangers in the next round.

Meanwhile in the UEFA Cup we had been drawn to play Ipswich, but any excitement that this draw created was somewhat overshadowed at the time by our terrible start to the League. First we played Dundee United away. They had changed their style of play and quite simply caught us cold. By playing the ball forward as soon as they got possession and pushing players up to support the frontrunners they gave us a real doing. We trailed 3-0 at half-time and although we recovered a bit in the second-half the final score was 4-1. But worse was to follow. In our first home League game, Celtic, with Nicholas, McCluskey and McGarvey — three players who were always a threat to us — beat us 3-1. I felt then that our youngsters, Black, Hewitt, Simpson, Cooper and Angus, were just a little bit overwhelmed.

We were due to play Ipswich away on 16 September. We knew that Bobby Robson had already been to watch us at Broomfield against Airdrie in our last League Cup section match when we played five reserves because we were already assured of a place in the next round. He was disappointed and had left at half-time. We had also been spying on Ipswich. Archie had seen them playing Liverpool at Anfield and Sunderland at home and we had both seen them playing Birmingham at Portman Road. We knew it was going to be a hard tie. Ipswich had just won the UEFA Cup and were a team packed with international and quality players. But the Liverpool experience had matured us. We felt we had learned a lot since then and when we beat Partick Thistle 2-0 the Saturday before the Ipswich game it gave us the League win we badly needed for our confidence.

Our tactics for the match at Ipswich were right. We played 4-4-2, with Strachan and Weir playing deep and wide so they could get to their full-backs and also tighten the midfield. This would mean that Muhren and Thyssen would have to move infield, where they would come up against the strength of Watson and Cooper. We played Rougvie against Mariner with Miller left free at the back.

The game went well for us. We had plenty of good possession and Strachan and Weir presented them with all sorts of problems. We had expected them to play the wee fellow Eric Gates but they left him out and played a normal front three. This meant that Cooper, who sat in front of the centre-backs, could take on John Wark's runs, and that

Willie Miller and Mick Mills shake hands before the match

Watson could move up in support of our strikers, McGhee and Hewitt. It was a good performance which we deserved to win, but at the end of the day to come away with a 1-1 draw was perfectly acceptable.

The return leg, of course, is history. Peter Weir absolutely destroyed them in the second-half at Pittodrie and it was a great night for Aberdeen. Those matches against Ipswich were tangible proof that we had learned in Europe. Our patience was getting better as was our possession of the ball and our belief in ourselves. Young players like Cooper and Simpson were once again outstanding. Cooper, of course, had already played quite a few games in the side and was fulfilling his early promise. Simpson, too, was proving to be a great asset. He is an honest and disciplined performer with a great appetite for the game as well as good stamina and excellent ball control.

I remember Bobby Robson being criticised after the game by the Scottish press for being a bad loser but I thought that was totally unfair. There are no great losers, though some can hide it. At the end of the day good managers like Bobby Robson are bad losers and don't take defeat well. I would probably have been the same if we had lost. Robson said he thought his team was unlucky and I understood his reasons for saying that whether he believed it or not. What he said was for the benefit of his own team, not for anyone else. Ipswich were top of the English League at the time and had a hard game against Southampton coming up on the Saturday. Their manager's priority was to make sure that they were ready to meet that challenge. In fact, I admired Robson for coming into our dressing room after the match to shake hands with Willie Miller and myself. He said, 'All the best. You'll win this Cup easily now.' He really believed that and so did we.

Meanwhile we got through our League Cup game against Berwick Rangers and were drawn to meet our great rivals, Dundee United, in the next stage. The rivalry between Aberdeen and Dundee United has been great over recent seasons. I would say that they are the one team in Scotland who can come to Pittodrie and win. The funny thing is that we can regularly travel to Tannadice and beat them. The record in all the games against Jim McLean's team since I came to Aberdeen is incredible. Over 38 games up to the end of season 1984-85, we've won 14 and they've won 13 and the other 11 have been drawn. Goals scored are 49 for us and 46 for United. There is nothing between the two teams. I've said for years now that the Aberdeen v United games are more intense and harder than the Old Firm matches in my time as a player. They are two superbly fit, well-organised and well-coached teams. It is always difficult when we play United and they obviously say the same about ourselves. We have probably the better League record against them but they always seem to do better in the Cups against us.

In October, 1981, they knocked us out of the League Cup again. We won the first leg at Tannadice and thought we'd done well with a Peter Weir goal, although we should have maybe been two or three up that night. Then we lost the return leg at Pittodrie. Peter Weir was carried off early in the game, we lost three terrible goals and United gave us a real doing at our ground.

Our League form, however, had picked up. After the two bad defeats at the start of the season, we staged a recovery. We won our next four games, beating Partick before we played Ipswich, and beating Hibs, then managed by our old friend, Bertie Auld, with a late Neil Simpson goal. We had always hated playing Partick when Bertie

McGhee in action against Ipswich

was the manager because he was so negative. I remember once when Thistle came to Pittodrie, where they always seemed to sneak a draw, they were awarded a corner kick near the end of the match. Bertie had Colin McAdam taking the corner and one striker, Jim Melrose, in the box. Everyone else was out of the box on the halfway line. He did exactly the same one day with Hibs. It was 0-0 and they were given a free kick. He had six players back and Jackie McNamara played it away at the corner flag. When they got a corner kick, they had one striker taking the flag kick and one in the penalty box and all the rest of the team outside the box. Half a dozen of them must have been on the halfway line. I'm always desperate to beat that type of negative approach, which is destroying the game, and in all honesty I think that Bertie was more suited to managing a team with small resources like Partick, where survival was all-important, rather than doing anything for a big club like Hibs. Anyway that late goal from Neil Simpson gave us great satisfaction. Next we beat Airdrie 4-0 and then Morton at home 2-0. We got a 0-0 draw at Ibrox and then we beat St Mirren at home and away, Andy Watson scoring two marvellous goals that day. We beat Dundee at home and were achieving a bit of continuity. Then we went to Celtic Park and lost 2-1. It was one of our best performances there. We played really well but lost.

In the UEFA Cup we were drawn in the second round against Arges Pitesti and we won the home leg 3-0 with goals from Strachan,

Weir and Hewitt. It was 3-0 at half-time. The strange thing was that they had dropped their international goalkeeper, a huge guy. They started off with a small lad in goal but they took him off at half-time and brought on the big giant. Significantly, we didn't score any more goals. But if we felt confident going to Rumania with a three-goal lead, we were to get one of the biggest frights you could ever imagine.

The lessons you learn in Europe! You think the world's rosy and you are going along great guns, then all of a sudden the roof falls in. That's what happened over in Rumania. We decided to play two wide, Peter Weir and Gordon Strachan, with Mark McGhee through the middle, just to keep things tight, give us a good width and also give us easy possession of the ball. But wee Gordon had such a bad first-half — he kept going away deep into midfield — I was going bananas. That prompted the famous incident at half-time when I threw a tray of cups at him as he answered me back. It was a spur of the moment thing, and fortunately none of the cups hit him — I still don't know how I missed him! I'm not proud of these events, but things happen on the spur of the moment. At least it motivated Gordon to improve himself in the second-half and from being 2-0 down at half-time we managed' to rescue a 2-2 draw. In actual fact we played quite well in the second-half and should have won.

In the third round our opponents were SV Hamburg. All the lessons about Liverpool, about possession of the ball, about taking chances, seemed to desert us in the first leg and if I've seen sure signs of insanity in a match they were shown that night, 25 November, at Pittodrie against Hamburg. We decided to play an early challenging game because teams like Hamburg want to get the ball at the back. They like to develop their game slowly and build up. With players like Beckenbauer in the team, they wanted time. So we worked particularly hard on closing down people early, on early defence. It was important, if we were to have belief in ourselves, that we had the ball more than the other team and the quicker we got the ball back the better.

Archie had been to see them play and with them using Beckenbauer as a sweeper we felt it was most important that we got at them early and didn't allow Beckenbauer's arrogance and confidence to spur his team-mates round him. I made tactical changes. I left out Dougie Bell, who was good in Europe, and played Simpson and Watson as my two centre midfield players. Neale Cooper had been badly injured on the Saturday at Easter Road and Alex McLeish was also out with an injury, so I had to play Doug Rougvie at centre-half. In fact, he did exceptionally well against big Hrubesch and hardly gave him a kick of the ball. It was one of our best ever performances in

Europe but we won the game only 3-2 due to two moments of what can only be described as insanity.

A throw out from Jim Leighton brought confusion between him and Stuart Kennedy and we lost a goal. Then we were down to ten men, with Doug Rougvie being carried off. Eight of our players touched the ball during this time and not one of them had the sense to kick it out of play to allow Cooper to come on as a sub. And, of course, Hamburg scored their second goal then, with about four minutes to go.

The events of that night were a bad blow to us and, in effect, ended our chances of a run in the UEFA Cup. Our form preceding the second leg was a little bit topsyturvy. Mark McGhee was going through a nightmare of a time — 23 games without scoring a goal — and the press weren't going to let him forget about it. His failure to score was obviously affecting him and I was trying to give him as much protection as I could. On the Saturday before going to Hamburg I still wasn't convinced as to how we were going to play in Germany but my more immediate concern was our visit to our bogey team, Morton. Almost inevitably we lost 2-1 and Mark had such a bad game at Cappielow that day, I decided to leave him out for the European match.

I picked a team playing 4-3-3, with Hewitt and Black, two young lads who had been improving all that season, as my strikers, and Peter Weir at outside-left. Then, during the night before the match, Peter Weir tore a nerve in his back. We took him to a specialist in the middle of the night, we took him to hospital the next day, we had him in traction, we tried everything. But Peter didn't make it and he was to be sorely missed. I probably at that point should have brought McGhee back into the team, moving Hewitt to the wing, but having made my decision about the strikers I decided to stick with it and reverted to 4-4-2, bringing Andy Watson into the midfield. It turned out to be a big mistake. Watson consistently gave the ball away too easily, Gordon Strachan had a really bad game and we had no composure at all. If you give the ball away in Europe, you're dead. That night we were killed. We lost 3-1 and ironically our scorer — a splendid goal as well — was our late substitute, Mark McGhee!

Bad weather then hit Scotland and broke whatever continuity the team had going. We took the players over to Spain for a break and played a friendly against Benidorm. Our next game was 23 January, a Scottish Cup tie against Motherwell at Fir Park where we were decidedly lucky to scrape a 1-0 victory in a match memorable only for John Hewitt's goal straight from the kick-off — 9.6 seconds to be exact! As fate would have it that scrappy game was to be the inauspicious start to a run of three Scottish Cup triumphs in succession, but that was the furthest thing from my mind when I emerged from the dressing room to meet the press and was informed we had been drawn against Celtic at home in the next round.

Although my public response to the news was 'That's fine by me', I knew Celtic in the Cup was going to be a difficult one for us. We had played them in a League match a few weeks before at Pittodrie when they had beaten us comprehensively with Nicholas in brilliant form. The week after the Motherwell match, in fact, they beat us convincingly again in a League match at Parkhead. The Cup tie was scheduled for 13 February and the omens for us were not good — we drew 0-0 with Partick Thistle in a midweek match on 3 February and then 0-0 at home to Morton on the Saturday before Celtic's visit. To add to our problems, we had Neale Cooper injured and Neil Simpson only beginning to recover from an injury — we obviously needed some strength in the middle of the park.

On the Monday morning I called the players in from training and told them we were going to change the playing system, that we had to change it to beat Celtic, and that if we beat Celtic we would win the Cup. I wanted to get the players out of the public gaze to prepare for the match — I felt that Billy McNeill and Celtic knew too many people in the Aberdeen area — so we spent the week preparing thoroughly at Woodside, behind closed doors.

On the day we played Alex McLeish in the middle of the park along with Neil Simpson and Gordon Strachan, with Doug Rougvie at centre-half and John McMaster at left-back. It came up trumps. McLeish was absolutely magnificent. We won 1-0 through a John Hewitt goal in a gritty Cup tie where we never gave Celtic the chance to settle. It proved to be a turning point for us — we went through the rest of the season's 22 games with only one defeat, against, inevitable though it may sound, Morton. The Greenock side's goal that day came late on in the match again. Leighton had just made a great save but the ball hit referee Brian McGinlay's heel, shot back towards goal and Rooney followed up to put it in the net!

In the Scottish Cup quarter final we went through 4-2, with Gordon Strachan scoring twice from the penalty spot in a bad-tempered game with Kilmarnock. We were next drawn against St Mirren in the semi-final at Parkhead in another controversial game. St Mirren had Abercromby sent off for a terrible tackle on Strachan, but then referee Hugh Alexander allowed Frank McDougall to bundle Jim Leighton to the ground and they scored from the resulting corner kick. Everyone was amazed that no foul had been given. We equalised with a Gordon Strachan penalty, a softish award and one of those decisions that make you think a referee is maybe trying to cancel out an earlier mistake. The replay at Dens Park was another gruelling game with the rain lashing down and the pitch in a bog-like condition. In a game famous for its goalkeeping mistakes and a really good advert for Cup football we won through 3-2 with Peter Weir, who had missed the first game through injury, scoring the winning goal against his old club. We would now face Rangers in the Final.

Meanwhile our League form was good and our goal rate was unbelievable. We scored three against Hibs at home, three against Rangers at Ibrox, three away to Dundee, beat Dundee United 2-1 at home, Celtic 1-0 away, Hibs 3-0 away, St Mirren 4-1 and 5-0, Dundee 5-0, Rangers at home 4-0, and Partick at home 3-1. Mark McGhee had found his touch again. His early season uncertainty had vanished and he was now playing well and scoring regularly. We were looking forward to this Cup Final with optimism and real belief in ourselves.

Our preparations for Cup Finals follow a standard pattern. If we have no injuries to cause delay to team selection we will announce the team to the players on the Monday. We have a Jacuzzi session on the Monday morning, followed by a team talk setting out our plans for the players so that they know exactly what's required — they know the team and they get on with the business. On the Tuesday we have a press day, when photographers and reporters can attend the training session at Pittodrie so that we don't need to see them for the rest of the week and so that they get enough material to last them the rest of the week. On the Wednesday we go to Cruden Bay where we have a morning training session, followed by lunch and then nine holes of golf. This helps the players relax away from Aberdeen and away from people hustling for tickets or interviews. On the Thursday we go to our favourite training ground at Woodside. We actually have a superstition about having to be there before a Cup tie and we prepare thoroughly there any new tactics for the big match. Friday is simply a matter of normal Friday preparation at Pittodrie for a Saturday match, going over the tactics in another team talk before leaving for the Excelsior Hotel in Glasgow where we usually stay the night.

We knew that Rangers were having their problems for that Cup Final. Their team was on the point of breaking up — Colin Jackson and Sandy Jardine were getting on in years and Peter McCloy was replaced for the Final by Jim Stewart. They also played Alex Miller out of position, in midfield. Nevertheless, we also knew that you could never treat Rangers lightly in a Cup Final. For our part we were missing Peter Weir through injury.

I decided to play a midfield of four with Gordon Strachan at half

73

shift from wide right into midfield and John McMaster on the left side of Neale Cooper and Neil Simpson. We started the game well. Our attitude was good, our belief was strong and we were playing positively. Just when I thought there was a bit of slackness among the Rangers players they scored a really good goal from a Dalziel cross and a McDonald header. They increased the pace of their game then and were beginning to cause us a few problems and I went down to the dugout to get John Hewitt to threaten Sandy Jardine more in the right-back's area. He was allowing Sandy too much room. Just when I reached the dugout from the stand we got the break we needed. A corner kick came out to Alex McLeish and he touched the ball to the side before bending a marvellous shot into Jim Stewart's top left-hand corner. We were back in the game.

At half-time I again lectured the players. 'Do you really want to win this Cup? You're not here just to make up the numbers. I've been through all this before about going to beat Celtic at Parkhead and Rangers at Ibrox, but can you do it in Cup Finals? That's the question. You've won the League, you've done well in some European games, but can you win Cup Finals?'

They answered that brilliantly themselves. Aberdeen put on a great second-half performance. In fact it was all against the run of play that the game needed to go to extra-time at all. The deciding factor in the match was when I replaced John McMaster with Dougie Bell, who absolutely destroyed Rangers on the left midfield. I also brought on Eric Black and his touch and lightness about the park improved things up front. We won 4-1 in extra-time but Rangers had well and truly lost the game long before the final whistle.

We'd done it! Winning a Cup Final is a great occasion because the whole country is watching. There is a tremendous build-up and a great atmosphere and Hampden is a special place. There is the presentation of the Cup and the honour for the players. There is also the intense satisfaction of knowing you've made at least 25,000 Aberdeen supporters in the Hampden crowd happy. People who've travelled from all over the country, from the far north, from Sutherland, from Orkney and Shetland and the islands. From country places like Alford, Huntly and Keith. It's marvellous to win for them and especially against the Old Firm because we've been beaten by them in the past.

And the best feeling of all was knowing that this was just the beginning. We had just missed the League by a point and we had won the Scottish Cup. It was a satisfying season by any standards but there was better to come. The younger players were improving. Strachan, McGhee, Weir, McLeish and Miller were all reaching their peak. The

74

understanding at the back of the defence was uncanny. Leighton was improving and developing and Stuart Kennedy was at his best. The team knew they were on the verge of something and everything seemed to go up a gear after we beat Rangers in that Cup Final. We knew there were balmy days ahead.

After the match we went to the Gleneagles Hotel in Perthshire to celebrate. There we met two truly big men of contrasting roles — Jock Wallace and Burt Lancaster! Burt was filming *Local Hero* in Scotland and met that night one of his greatest fans in Stuart Kennedy. Stuart received a personal invitation to meet the film star in his suite and proceeded to amaze the American by reeling off all the roles Burt had played in his films. Later the star came down to meet all the players and congratulate them. Congratulations came also from Big Jock Wallace who joined us for a drink. He was managing Leicester at the time and was up in Scotland for the weekend. But knowing Jock's love for Rangers we didn't press him too hard for his opinion of our victory!

It was a great night. Archie Knox was grandly signing bills with the chairman's name and I remember buying one round of drinks that came to £90. Unabashed, I simply appended my signature — R M Donald! I don't know what the total bill came to at the end of the night but the chairman laughed it off later in the week — after he'd recovered.

The players celebrate the 4-1 Scottish Cup victory over Rangers

To top a good season, another great satisfaction to us was the growing recognition of our players for the international team. Four were selected for Scotland's World Cup squad in Spain — Leighton, McLeish, Miller and Strachan. It was a treat for me to go to Spain and watch my players perform on the highest stage of all — the World Cup Finals. People talk about players being world-class and that's a much-abused term. The only way you can judge whether a player is world-class is if they perform well on the World Cup stage. Willie Miller and Gordon Strachan did that in Spain.

Directors and families with the Scottish Cup

PREMIER DIVISION CHAMPIONSHIP

	P	W	L	D	F	A	Pts
CELTIC	36	24	5	7	79	33	55
ABERDEEN	36	23	6	7	71	29	53
RANGERS	36	16	9	11	57	45	43
DUNDEE UNITED	36	15	11	10	61	38	40
ST MIRREN	36	14	13	9	49	52	37
HIBERNIAN	36	11	11	14	38	40	36
MORTON	36	9	15	12	31	54	30
DUNDEE	36	11	21	4	46	72	26
PARTICK THISTLE	36	6	20	10	35	59	22
AIRDRIE	36	5	23	8	31	76	18

SCOTTISH CUP

Third Round	Motherwell	Away	W	1-0	
Fourth Round	Celtic	Home	W	1-0	
Fifth Round	Kilmarnock	Home	W	4-2	
Semi-final	St Mirren	Parkhead	D	1-1	
Replay	St Mirren	Dens	W	3-2	
Final	Rangers	Hampden	W	4-1	AET

LEAGUE CUP

Qual. Sect.	Kilmarnock	Home	W	3-0
	Hearts	Away	L	0-1'
	Airdrie	Home	W	3-0
	Hearts	Home	W	3-0
	Kilmarnock	Away	W	3-0
	Airdrie	Away	D	0-0
Q-final 1st leg	Berwick	Home	W	5-0
2nd leg	Berwick	Away	W	3-0
S-final 1st leg	Dundee United	Away	W	1-0
2nd leg	Dundee United	Home	L	0-3

UEFA CUP

1st R 1st leg	Ipswich Town	Away	D	1-1	
2nd leg	Ipswich Town	Home	W	3-1	4-2
2nd R 1st leg	Arges Pitesti	Home	W	3-0	
2nd leg	Arges Pitesti	Away	D	2-2	5-2
3rd R 1st leg	SV Hamburg	Home	W	3-2	
2nd leg	SV Hamburg	Away	L	1-3	4-5

Top Scorer: Gordon Strachan 17

Chapter Five
1982-83: European Glory

ANOTHER SUMMER passed and as usual I was desperate to get the new season started. We had no contractual problems — our main players were still on four-year contracts — and no one wanted to leave the club. The players in the World Cup squad were told that they could have their holidays extended and that they could report two weeks after we had started training.

One of the great aspects of Aberdeen Football Club is its association with the Highland League teams and its relationships with clubs north of the oil capital itself. That pre-season we made an excellent tour up north, playing against Ross County, Nairn County, Inverness Thistle and an Invergordon Select, to open a new ground. We paraded the Scottish Cup with us and it proved to be a great public relations exercise — people loved it and made us very welcome everywhere.

Our northern tour, together with our usual week at Gordonstoun, sharpened us up for the season. But first we played Ipswich at Pittodrie in a testimonial for Drew Jarvie in front of a most disappointing crowd of only 8,700. I'm not sure I know the reason for that low turnout — possibly non-competitive friendlies at that time of the year, with many people still on holiday, just have no drawing power. Nevertheless I felt sorry for Drew, who had given the club marvellous service.

Jarvie was popular with the Aberdeen players who regarded him as the old maestro. His nickname at the club was 'Crime Count' as it was fairly obvious that he would fall foul of referees from time to time. But he was another player I had a lot of time and respect for, a hard battler and exceptional in the sense that he could more or less guarantee an average of between 12 and 18 goals a season from midfield. As his remark at Anfield when we were 3-0 down showed, he was also a player who never gave up. I'm glad to see he's now doing so well as a coach at St Mirren.

Our first competitive game that season was in the League Cup against Morton at Cappielow. We drew 2-2 when we should have won.

The following Saturday we drew 3-3 at Pittodrie in a ding-dong League Cup tie with Dundee, which we felt relieved to get a point out of. Then it was time for an early start in Europe where the European Cup-Winners' Cup draw had paired us with Sion of Switzerland in a preliminary round.

As we approached our home leg with Sion the players were constantly reminded of how we had destroyed our chances against Hamburg the previous season. The lesson sunk in so well we annihilated the Swiss team 7-0 in the first game. Perhaps the strangest sight of that night, though, came after the match, for the Sion manager Donze believed in training his players *after* a game — something I'd never seen done before — and there they were going through their paces under the Pittodrie floodlights in an empty stadium. When we went to Switzerland for the return leg we played in the most picturesque setting for any stadium I've ever seen, with a backdrop of mountains brightly lit at night by the house lights of the various hamlets. We were relaxed and comfortable with a seven-goal cushion and won the second leg by 4-1.

We came back to start the League programme against Dundee United at Tannadice and lost 2-0 in a match where we didn't play well at all. From there we concentrated on sorting out the weaknesses and beat Morton at home the next week — two in a row against Morton without losing! We went to Love Street next and were unlucky to draw 1-1, then Rangers came to Pittodrie and beat us — their first victory at Pittodrie in the Premier League. The Rangers supporters stayed in the ground chanting for about forty-five minutes after the game ended. You'd have thought they'd won the World Cup, but then again that was a measure of how much Aberdeen had improved. Their celebration was also a recognition of our achievement. In actual fact it was a game in which we were struck with injuries and were unlucky to go down by 2-1.

Meanwhile we had progressed in the League Cup, winning our section easily enough, only to be knocked out by Dundee United in the two-leg quarter final, losing both games 3-1 and 1-0. In the first game we actually started well and were 1-0 ahead when Bannon hit a thirty-yard shot that no one even saw. It was all downhill from there: we lost the tie and went out of the tournament. But our League form held up with a 3-1 victory over Celtic at Parkhead setting up a good run in which we beat Dundee, Kilmarnock and Dundee United, dropping a point to Hibs on the way. Our form was without doubt on the way up when we were drawn to face Dinamo Tirane, an unknown Albanian team, in the next round of the Cup-Winners' Cup.

Unknown they remained too until they turned up at Pittodrie, for Albanian officialdom created all sorts of problems with visas and we couldn't travel over to watch them play beforehand. We scraped through that first leg at Pittodrie 1-0 with a John Hewitt goal but it was a decidedly unsatisfactory performance. I must say, though, the Albanian team loved Scotland. We had booked them into a good hotel and shown them traditional Scottish hospitality. The aspect that they seemed to enjoy most was being able to order steaks for breakfast!

For our part, we took food parcels to Albania, not knowing what to expect and unwilling to leave anything to chance, but I must say they returned our hospitality in full. For the game itself the pitch was in beautiful condition and the only problem was the intense heat of 92 degrees. The longer the game went on the more I wondered if our players would last out. It was, however, the Albanians who tired first. Our stamina proved itself over the 90 minutes and it was a good performance on our part as far as possession football was concerned. We drew 0-0 in a game we should have won but we were through to the next round.

Lech Poznan of Poland were to be our next opponents in the tournament, so I sent Archie Knox out to have a look at them. It was at the time of the Gdansk troubles and Archie was to find himself accompanied everywhere by a man whom he could only presume to be from the secret police. Archie's new friend even insisted on sharing Archie's room at night and I can assure you Archie looked tired when he got home! He moaned about it for weeks and later on in the tournament we had a laugh when we pretended we'd been drawn for the quarter finals against the Russian team and told Archie to start making plans for his visa. He immediately threatened to resign. Anyway, we beat the Polish team 2-0 at Pittodrie with second-half goals from McGhee and Weir and over there we played great possession football and clinched the tie with a Doug Bell header.

One of the great things about the European Cup-Winners' Cup or the European Champions Cup is that you know who you will be playing against as early as December and have time to prepare for the game in March. You can have your opponents watched as many times as you need to. The quarter final draw for the Cup-Winners' Cup had matched us with the mighty Bayern Munich and that brought an excitement to Pittodrie which we had never witnessed or experienced before. We immediately operated the voucher system so that our regular supporters would get a chance to see the second-leg tie and there was an obvious increase in crowds over the Christmas and New Year games. We beat Hibs 2-0 and Kilmarnock 2-0, both games at home and both with crowds of around 19,000 — well up on previous years.

In January I went over to see Bayern play at Karlsruhe where they won 6-0. It started to snow during the game and it became a bit of a farce. Bayern Munich played fairly well and were up 3-0 after 15 minutes but to be honest I was astounded at the poor standard of play by Karlsruhe. People often talk about the high standard of German football and although it is possible that a very high standard is produced by teams like Bayern Munich and Hamburg, some of the others are very, very poor. I took my usual notes and I was sure we had a few things to sort out — namely Rummenigge and Breitner. Archie had also gone to see them when they again won 6-0 and it was obvious that they were a very good side with very good professionals. Three players who also impressed us were the full-back Dremmler whom I consider to be a tremendous player, a real battler with a tremendous attitude, Augenthaler, one of their centre-backs or sweeper as we would call him, and their goalkeeper, Pfaff, although it turned out that he did not play against us.

Although Breitner was reaching the twilight of his career, he had played in the World Cup Finals and we knew how big a threat he was going to be to us. As for Rummenigge, he was obviously going to be difficult to handle. We toyed with the idea of man-marking him because one minute he plays in midfield and the next minute he is acting as an out-and-out striker. We decided that if he came into midfield, then our midfield would cope with him and if he came into the front line of attack then Willie Miller would take him. As for Breitner, Neale Cooper was going to look after him once he approached the halfway line.

Unfortunately we did not have Gordon Strachan for the first leg at Munich, so we started off with a midfield of Simpson, Cooper and Bell with Black, McGhee and Weir up front. Our whole preparation was based on the fact that this was going to be a real testing ground and that we had learned from experience in the previous year after throwing away the tie against Hamburg. This was to be an acid test for us. Much of our tactical talk centred round holding on to the ball and I also discussed with Peter Weir how to handle the right-back, how he would have to give Dremmler plenty to do to stop his surging runs. Of course, at the end of the day, when you get to this level of the game you have to hope that everyone will play well on the night.

It is history now, but we really played tremendously well — probably our best away performance in Europe. We dominated the middle of the park and although there were odd flashes from

Rummenigge, Willie Miller was always magnificent. The players took a lead from Miller's performance. The support was also tremendous on the night and they were all convinced that we were on our way to the semi-final. I was excited about the situation and the players were affected too. The Press were already anticipating that we could be in a semi-final, but deep down I knew about the hard job which was still to be done and I told the players they had to appreciate that they must achieve even more in the return leg.

For the second match, I decided to leave Doug Bell on the bench, mainly because Gordon Strachan was fit again and it was going to be his type of night. The atmosphere in the stadium was tremendous. But Bayern got a grip of the game from the start and played a come and catch us approach. If they got themselves into trouble, they would play it back to the free player at the back or even back to the goalkeeper. This is a tactic which Aberdeen themselves have used over the years to try and take the steam out of a game. Then, of course, Bayern scored from a free kick. I did not agree that it was a foul since it was a very soft clash between Alex McLeish and big Dieter Honness. Nevertheless, Breitner tapped the ball and Augenthaler scored with a tremendous shot. That goal silenced the crowd immediately and it took us about fifteen minutes to get going again.

In our pre-match tactical meetings, we talked about adversity and about losing a goal, and how to handle it. But on the night, we didn't handle the loss of that goal well. For a while we stuttered along. We needed a break, we needed a spark of genius from someone. Our goal, when it finally came, had a bit of spark about it. From a good move involving Kennedy, Strachan and McGhee on the right-hand side, a deep cross came over from Mark McGhee to the far post. Eric Black got to it and knocked it back somehow for Neil Simpson to come charging in. He clashed with one of the defenders on the line and pushed it into the net. So that was us on level terms and, in the next minute, Eric Black's header hit the bar. We were right on song but unfortunately the first-half was at an end.

At half-time we discussed the situation and agreed that we had given away a bad goal. To win things you have to defend well. It is a principle we have followed throughout. Having players like Leighton, McLeish and Miller is a base to operate from and their soundness at the back has given us freedom to attempt things up front. It allows us to throw people forward, knowing that we have as secure a back three as you will ever find in Europe. But as they often say about big games, to win you have to go through the agonies. We certainly went through our share that night.

A few minutes after half-time, they scored again. A cross from the little winger Del-Haye, who had been giving Rougvie a terrible time, was deflected out by Alex McLeish to the big lad Pflugler, who was being used as a tactical ploy to stop the smaller Stuart Kennedy going forward. He hit a tremendous volley from about 20 yards and at that stage my gut feeling told me that we had had it. Time was beginning to run out — now we were trailing 2-1 with only 30 minutes to score two goals.

I had done a lot of thinking before the game and was doing a lot of thinking on the bench that night with regard to the alternatives with my substitutions, how to use them, who could react to going a goal behind. It was certainly a time for gambling because I thought we were out of the game and out of the Cup. Bayern were looking comfortable and their goalkeeper was making some tremendous saves, one in particular from an Eric Black header. I knew that I had to gamble. I had to get someone on who could get behind them from deeper, who could change the variety in the middle of the park. Although Gordon Strachan was getting a little bogged down, he still had the spark which he always has the potential to produce. I obviously had to keep him on and I also had to retain the grit of Simpson and Cooper, who possess qualities you need in these types of games. The only problems which I really faced were with the two full-backs. Doug Rougvie was having a nightmare of a match and Stuart Kennedy was having an uncomfortable night against the big fellow Pfluger, who was winning a lot of balls in the air and of course had also scored their second goal. I decided to put John McMaster on to midfield to allow him to use his precision passes and I moved Neale Cooper to left-back where I felt he would handle the wee winger better. Then I moved Doug Rougvie to right-back where I felt he could better use his height. It was obviously an unpopular substitution to take Kennedy off and I remember the crowd reacting pretty badly. They couldn't believe it. To the crowd he was a hero and a marvellous player but on this occasion it warranted the change. When you have substitutes and you've got to take a chance, you have to make decisions and be brave about them.

John McMaster came on and immediately made an impact on the game with his variety and his use of the ball. He can play a short or a long pass and introduced a good left foot into the game. Things started to improve for us although we still could not get the breakthrough. I then had to use my second substitute and I decided to put John Hewitt on. John is a tremendous substitute and although he lacks the consistency for a full game, he can come on and change a match and often score. Some players are not good substitutes, they are not used to it mainly because they take a long time to get warmed up and cannot get into the swing of the game, but John Hewitt is excellent in this role. I decided to put him on and took a pure gamble by taking Neil Simpson off. Neil had run himself to a standstill and had done a marvellous job. We pulled Peter Weir back to left midfield where he could still be useful and we then played a front three of Eric Black, Mark McGhee and John Hewitt. It was certainly a mad gamble, but as I have often said before, if you want to win games, you have to be brave. There was a European trophy at stake and I was prepared to take any gamble to get us into the semi-final that night.

Just after we brought John Hewitt on, we were awarded a free kick outside the penalty box. John McMaster and Gordon Strachan had operated our free kicks for a number of years and they used to have a ploy at corner kicks where the opposition did not know if it was to be the right foot or the left foot. That worked well for a while but it was stopped by the SFA. We operated the same system with free kicks where two players run over the ball as if one of them had missed and as one of them ran back, either Gordon Strachan or John McMaster whipped it into the penalty box. It certainly worked that night. All the Bayern players were flummoxed and the free kick was turned in by an Alex McLeish header which brought the score to 2-2.

In the next minute we got the winner. Neale Cooper took the throw on the left-hand side of the park to John McMaster, who took two touches of the ball and hit a marvellous back post cross for Eric Black to get a header in. Their goalkeeper somehow managed to get a hold of it but only managed to push it down. The ball dropped to John Hewitt who came in and scored the winning goal. The crowd were absolutely delirious. Two minutes before that, we were out of the Cup and now we were winning 3-2 and into the semi final.

The legs had gone from Bayern. Breitner was hobbling about, Augenthaler was injured and the only one who was still a potential problem was Rummenigge. The wee winger was getting stiffer attention from Neale Cooper. But there were still thirteen minutes to go and I was worried stiff in case they scored an equaliser. If they did, we were out on the away goals rule. I was now left with a midfield of Strachan, McMaster and Weir and neither of them was a particularly powerful tackler. Up front, Eric Black was tiring badly. I had to depend on my back four to do their job, together, of course, with Jim Leighton should he be required. Thankfully the only problem was an overhead kick from Rummenigge which Leighton saved well. We lasted out and in the end it was a marvellous night for the Aberdeen supporters.

It was only in the dressing room that we realised how close we were to getting into the Final. If we had lost that night, we would have said, 'Well we were two games away from the Final.' Now, suddenly, when we were there, in the semi-finals, we realised how close the Final was. A few days after the game, the manager at the Skean Dhu Hotel at Altens told me that the Bayern players who were staying at the hotel sat in the lounge and could not believe that we had planned that particular free kick. It was obviously a tremendous disappointment for them because with only fifteen minutes to go, they were in the semi-finals. We had really kicked them in the gut.

But although all the euphoria surrounded that night at Pittodrie when we won, it was our tactical performance in the first leg where we got away with a no-scoring draw that was crucial. All the work that went into the preparation of the first leg paid off and the result had given us the confidence to attack the second leg. Nevertheless, it was a tremendous performance from Aberdeen. That night was the coming of age in Europe and it gave the players the belief that they really could win the European Cup-Winners' Cup Final. On the night, we had not committed suicide as we did against Hamburg the previous year, we did not make the same mistakes.

In the semi-final draw we were paired with Waterschei while the other semi-final was between Real Madrid and Austria Memphis. Archie and I both went to Belgium to have a look at them. We were impressed with their fluid 4-2-4, 4-4-2 system. I felt, however, the biggest problem might be their manager who was a shrewd, wiry fellow called Ernst Kunecke. He had changed Waterschei fortunes within the last two or three years. They had been down in one of the lower divisions, then gained promotion to the first division and here they were now in the semi-final of a European tournament in which they had beaten some good sides. It was a team which we could not underestimate.

Unfortunately, our League performance was beginning to suffer slightly because the Aberdeen players became obsessed in anticipation of the important European semi-final. They knew what was at stake but it was unknown ground that they were to be covering. Obviously other games became side issues. Probably the players' whole lives became side issues for a short time and certainly during that period of League matches, their minds were not completely on the games.

In the first leg of the European Cup-Winners' Cup semi-final at Pittodrie we found that Waterschei, as we expected, were inclined to pull their left-back in to mark players in order to allow the right-back, a Hungarian international, Macra, to move up. This allowed their sweeper to play in behind the two centre-backs. To counter that system, we decided to play Peter Weir more as a left midfield player and Gordon Strachan further up on the right to ensure that they had to play with a left-back. I also decided to leave Neale Cooper out and I brought in Doug Bell along with Neil Simpson. Although that was never our best combination — there was a bit of an imbalance with Bell and Simpson playing together — we felt that it would be right for that night.

Bell had one of these nights that he reserves only for European Cup ties. He tore the heart out of the Waterschei midfield and laid the foundations for a tremendous performance. We scored as early as the second minute after a great run by Bell. He tore up the left-hand side, put over a square ball and Eric Black duly obliged. We had spoken before the game and were determined to put them under tremendous pressure at the beginning and not to allow them to settle and play as they were used to in Belgian football. Neil Simpson then won the ball from them out of their defence, beat two of them and put in a marvellous second goal. We could have been up more than 2-0 at half-time but to their credit, they dug in. Believe me they were a very good side — not many teams would have recovered from the two very quick goals, but they did recover and hung on into the game until half-time.

The second-half was a great ding-dong battle because they came out and opened up and could have scored two or three times. Fortunately, we managed to get a third goal after a great Doug Bell run and pass which Mark McGhee put home. That more or less sealed our victory but the question of goal difference is always important in Europe so we had to look for goals while ensuring that we did not lose any at the back. I brought on Neale Cooper after they scored to make it 3-1. We went on to score two further goals to make it 5-1 at full-time. The fifth goal resulted from a mêlée in front of the goal, where Mark McGhee finally scored at the fourth attempt.

We had achieved a great victory and were now confident that we would get to the Final. There was a great atmosphere at Pittodrie that night. Both the crowd and the team rose to the occasion. How many teams could win a semi-final 5-1?

The second leg of the Waterschei semi-final, though, was a great disappointment and not just because of the 1-0 scoreline against us. Towards the end of the game Stuart Kennedy caught his studs at the edge of the park and suffered a knee injury. No one realised it at the time, but that was to be his last game as an active player for the club. At any rate we were now definitely in the Final — a great achievement in itself.

Next morning I left Belgium on a direct flight to Madrid to watch

Stuart Kennedy

their second-leg match against Austria Memphis. Real Madrid came through to join us in the Final comfortably enough but, although it was a wet night and the match was played on heavy ground, I saw nothing much about their team to worry me. On my return to my hotel after the game I telephoned Archie Knox and the chairman and told them much the same thing. I remember saying to Archie: 'Don't tell anybody but, believe me, what a chance we've got!' I really believed that we could beat Real Madrid.

I later sent Archie out to Spain to watch Real playing against Valencia away from home. To this day I really do not know if it was intentional on their part, but Archie was certainly messed about on that trip. The promised ticket was not left for him at his hotel and after an hour or so of hassle at the stadium he managed to bribe a policeman to let him in, by which time of course there was only 25 minutes of the match left to play. Naturally enough Archie learned next to nothing in that time, although Valencia did beat them to avoid relegation. But a feeling was growing between Archie and myself that we could beat Real Madrid. We were sure because our own form was good, the players we had were good, and although Gordon Strachan had a slight hamstring injury and was causing us a wee bit of concern, we knew that the big occasion would bring out the best in him.

In the Scottish Cup we had beaten Celtic in the semi-final prior to the Waterschei second leg and it was just as well that we had a 5-1 lead in the European competition because during part of the semi-final at Hampden we had only eight men on the park. Celtic adopted what for them was an unusually aggressive and physical approach to the game. But we were a far superior side to them that day, although we won by the only goal of the match through Peter Weir who had just recovered from injury and had come on as a second-half substitute.

By that time we felt that we had really thrown away our chance of the Premier League Championship. In March we had lost an important home match to Dundee United, then we lost to Rangers at Ibrox and then to St Mirren. That losing streak really should have hammered the nail into our coffin but then we hit a winning run in the League against Celtic, Motherwell and Hibs before turning in a champagne 5-0 performance against Kilmarnock in a League match brought forward to the Thursday night in order to give us a week to prepare for our European Final. That match left us a point behind Dundee United and level with Celtic. Dundee United's last match was at Dens Park while ourselves and Celtic each had home matches as our last game. All three leaders were to win their important games but as history records, Dundee United lifted their first ever Premier League Championship.

However, with Peter Weir back to full fitness and Gordon Strachan improving by the day we began to look forward to the European Cup-Winners' Cup Final more perhaps then we had a few weeks before during a spate of injuries. After the Thursday night game against Kilmarnock I gave the players the Friday and Saturday off as rest days. We had arranged a Sunday game at Easter Road against Hibs Reserves, really to give Dougie Bell and Eric Black a try-out for fitness. Archie took them down with the reserves while I took the first team squad for a training session.

There was an exuberance about the training that Sunday and I just knew if I could get Bell and Black both declared fit, I could have the choice of the team I wanted. In fact choosing the team would be my biggest dilemma. As it was, Bell didn't pass the test and Black did. That was a personal tragedy for Dougie because he had contributed so much to our European run that year but had to miss the Final completely. But in a way the fact that Bell didn't make it and Stuart Kennedy couldn't make it relieved me of my problem. The team now more or less picked itself. A back four of Rougvie, Miller, McLeish and McMaster; a midfield of Strachan, Simpson and Cooper; and upfront McGhee, Black and Weir.

On the Sunday I also brought the players' wives in for a talk. Despite all the players' mumblings about how their wives would soon tell me a thing or two and their threats of what the women would say to me, their wives were as good as gold about the situation. I told them that this was the greatest occasion ever for the players and if they had any problems with regard to their husbands to see me. I asked them to try to give their husbands as much help as possible, to try not to cause undue problems as the players would already be nervous and edgy. Above all, to try and understand what was going on — the greatest day in a player's life, playing in a European Cup Final against the greatest European team of all. I also sent the players' wives the itinerary for the trip to Gothenburg and in it were joke items, making out as if they were going off to an army camp — palliasses, sleeping bags, tin mugs and the like. It went down well because later, at one of the supporters' functions, I was presented with a gift of a sleeping bag!

Everything felt right. The atmosphere among the players was positive and the build-up was good. Thanks to a friend of mine who is a security boss of Volvo trucks we also had the right hotel and training facilities in the Gothenburg area. Although we had been offered the training camp used by the international teams, his advice was not to take it, that it was too Spartan. We decided to stay in a place called Farsaat, which seemed to have been named especially for someone accustomed to the Doric — 'whar's at?' It was in a small hamlet called Kungalv outside Gothenburg and we had access to a beautiful training ground at an amateur club there. The rooms were not luxurious but the food was excellent.

We flew from Aberdeen on the Monday. We usually like to fly out on a Tuesday before a Wednesday game so we have less time in a strange place and we get back as quickly as possible, but it was a European Final and there was more media attention than ever. We felt that the proper thing to do was to go out there on the Monday, get ourselves settled in, and try to relax as much as possible. Our plane was full of the usual supporters and a more than usual representation from the press. The airport were giving out rosettes and the players received a singing telegram from their wives before we set out. It was a carnival of excitement, and we were on our merry way.

I decided, and I told Archie, to play it as low key as possible. Relax and make sure that none of the staff showed any nerves whatsoever. It was important we didn't affect anything in the players' build-up. These things you learn from your experience as a manager. You know when sometimes to look nervous, to look a wee bit anxious in order to communicate apprehension to the players and get them motivated properly. I look upon every game as being important and sometimes in the small games I do use a certain amount of psychology — I try to create something out of nothing. As if it is a harder game than it should be. But they could handle the big games now and I felt relaxed. I was sure they could handle Real Madrid.

Next day we trained at the stadium where the match would be played. All the press were there and Real Madrid were due to use the park after us. We did a thorough and varied session whereas Real Madrid came in and just practised penalty kicks. That gave us a sign of their own intentions. There was a feeling that they would maybe try to play for penalty kicks.

I got plenty of tips from Jock Stein which were important at the time. Jock was in the party with us and was eager to help me in any way he could and of course with his experience — having won the European Cup with Celtic — he was invaluable and I was delighted to listen to him. I even brought whisky for Stefano the Real Madrid manager. Stefano appreciated it.

On the Wednesday morning, as was our usual practice before an evening game, we took the players for a light training session, at the small amateur ground nearby, before packing them off to bed in the afternoon. In my team talk the previous night I was really positive in everything we spoke about and I made sure that we didn't praise any of the Real Madrid players. At that stage we didn't know if Stielike was going to be fit — they hadn't announced their side — but the feeling was that he would play. We pointed out that even if he did play it would be his first match for seven or eight weeks and he wouldn't be properly prepared for a match of this nature. (How wrong can you be!) The rest of their players didn't worry us because we knew roughly how they played and what we had to do. Certainly Galligo could play a bit in the middle of the park but we had the players to handle him around there. With Simpson and Cooper, Strachan and Weir, the balance of the team was right. My only secret worry was that I never ever thought of Doug Rougvie as a right-back. He seemed to be more suited to the left-back area. But as it turned out Big Doug was a significant player on the night.

The team-talk centred largely round everything we had learned from previous matches in Europe. Then, to keep things active, we had a quiz with the players broken into four or five teams. Inevitably the arguments started over whether it was Hamilton Academicals or Hamilton Academical and so on, but it kept the spirit lighthearted and acted as a great distraction from the pressures the players might otherwise feel.

Of course the players were not the only ones feeling the pressure. Archie and I used our own friendly rivalry as a distraction. Every Friday in the season we had our own little football competition called 'Tips' in the gym. Now, as we were both keen joggers, I said, 'Right, let's have a race round the castle' — maybe three or four miles from our hotel and back. The players swore we were off our heads but it was all done just to keep things in the squad active.

After our afternoon sleep we woke up to find that the heavens had opened and it was bucketing down. This, of course, didn't do us any harm but people who say that conditions suited Aberdeen that night are only partially correct. I've always felt that heavy conditions don't necessarily suit players like John McMaster, Gordon Strachan or Eric Black. The difference that night was going to be the will to win, not the weather. The hunger to do well is the most important factor and we certainly had it then.

Our support that night was magnificent, absolutely great. 12,000 Aberdeen supporters, many of whom had begged and borrowed to be there. And the special thing about these people, for Aberdeen and for the whole of Scotland, was that they were good-natured and good-humoured. They were enjoying themselves and the people of Gothenburg were enjoying them. They were terrific ambassadors. Five hundred of them had even travelled by boat, the *St Clair*, and captured the public imagination. I had been at the quayside to see them off, just as Mark McGhee and I would be there to see them return. The stories of those 'boat people' have now entered Aberdeen folklore and my personal favourite is the one about the keepy-uppy competition where the winner reached the grand total of four! But even there, as so often happens to those who deserve it least, tragedy struck with the death of the young boy Philip Goodbrand who collapsed at the game. That was the only sour note of a wonderful night which I and many others will never forget.

The Final itself now seems like a dream. We got off to a tremendous start with a great Eric Black volley in the first few minutes of the game. Imagine young Eric's disappointment when the ball beat the goalkeeper only to hit the crossbar. Undismayed, though, Eric scored to put us one goal up in the eighteenth minute. Within ten minutes the game was level but all the patient coaxing about handling adversity and recovering from mistakes paid off that night, especially in the case of Alex McLeish who made the bad pass back that allowed Santillo into the box where Leighton had no option but to concede a penalty. After that one mistake big Alex just got better and better, as if the mistake had simply pushed him up a gear, made him more alive and aware. Considering he knew that his error could possibly have cost us the game, he really went on to make a marvellous contribution. He never put another foot wrong.

Eric Black scores the first goal of the European Cup-Winners' Cup Final

Tension on the bench

At the end of the first-half I felt that the main problem we had was that Stielike was being given too much space to play and despite our dismissal of him in our tactics talk he was turning out to be an eye opener. He was absolutely magnificent on the night and a great influence on his team. He was the one player in the Real team whom we couldn't defeat on the night, the one that kept them alive and kept urging them on. To combat Stielike Archie and I urged our two strikers to work back towards the game more quickly in order to squeeze Stielike forward towards Neale Cooper who was playing in front of our back four. I also told Peter Weir to move forward more often and to take their right-back with him.

The second-half was a transformation. Weir tore them apart, as a winger rather than a midfielder, and McGhee and Black started to work hard at coming back up the park. Stielike was given considerably less room and we were beginning to run over the top of them. But we still couldn't score again and the game went into extra-time.

That period worried me. I was remembering all the reports of how the Real Madrid players had spent most of their last training session taking penalty kicks and I really dreaded the match being decided that

John Hewitt scores . . .

. . . and celebrates

way. I put on John Hewitt for the injured Eric Black and then very nearly substituted Andy Watson for John Hewitt to give us more pace in the middle of the park. Then Weir beat two men down the line and chipped a beautiful cross to Mark McGhee. I can still see McGhee taking on their substitute and then whipping it into the centre for Hewitt to beat Stielike to the cross and head the ball into the net. A wonderful moment! The rest of the game couldn't go by quickly enough. Mark McGhee broke through again just shortly after and only the goalkeeper's legs stopped the ball bursting the net. Then they were given a free kick from a scoring position when we already made it time up. They took it before the referee blew and it was ordered to be retaken. Just prior to that second free kick big Bryan Gunn, our reserve goalkeeper who was sitting beside me on the bench, got down on his knees and said, 'Dear God, please let them miss it.' I loved him for that. The ball whistled past and the referee blew for full-time.

Our dugout erupted. I remember slipping and falling as I got off my seat but all the rest of them — Knoxie, Roland the physio, Teddy Scott and all the substitutes — just ran right over the top of me! I struggled to my feet with my clothes soaking and ran on to the park to hug Willie Miller.

When we got back to the dressing rooms there was a certain air of unreality. There were two Aberdeen rooms in the stadium's dressing room complex — one for the players and one for the directors, manager, coach and backroom boys. The players were singing and dancing in their room but our room was surprisingly quiet, as if we couldn't believe it — we'd beaten Real Madrid in a European Final. It's a strange thing but you feel quite humble at a moment of such triumph. You also feel a bit of sympathy for the losing team on such a big occasion. That is the way with Aberdeen Football Club in general. Chairman Dick Donald is not one to get carried away and generates a proper sense of humility throughout the club. One of the hardest and most important facets of my job now is to make sure it stays that way.

Then it was out of the room and into the magical whirlwind. Our wives and families were all there at a post-match reception upstairs, although we waited for Willie Miller and Gordon Strachan to return from the mandatory dope test. The press were shouting for quotes, the cameras were clicking and the television lights were flashing. There seemed to be bodies everywhere. We were no longer a team and a club but a series of fragmented groupings, some players talking to their wives, some to supporters, some still at the dope test. Old friends appeared and new friends arrived. The occasion engulfed us and we submitted happily. Orjan Persson, an old team-mate of mine from my

Willie Miller is presented with the European Cup-Winners' Cup

Rangers playing days, was one of the old friends who joined us for the reception. He raved about our team performance and how the Scottish game had changed since our playing days.

After the celebrations at the ground we returned to the hotel where Cathy and I, my brother Martin, my pal John Donachie and his wife, Archie Knox's brother, an old friend from Dunfermline John Grieve and his pals and George Ramsay and his wife were all in the mood to celebrate. It was also Maureen Ramsay's birthday so for her it was a double celebration. When we arrived at the hotel from the stadium all the supporters who were staying there had lined up to welcome us. Again they seemed to be in the distance to me. It was a strange feeling. Martin and John came forward to hug me and at last the ice was broken. I finally began to relax.

The rest of the night went smoothly. After a buffet meal and a few speeches we all broke into our groups as is the normal fashion. The staff, myself, and our wives along with my friends sat together and drank champagne throughout the night. But although I enjoyed the champagne I never let it get the better of me. I wanted to retain my faculties. I didn't want to forget.

John McMaster decides to wear it!

The night wore on and one by one the party broke up till only Teddy Scott, Cathy and I were left. It was after six in the morning and it was somehow fitting that the three of us should be the party's last survivors. Cathy, who has sacrificed a normal family life in support of me and has suffered a hard life married to a football manager, and Teddy. What can you say about this man that could adequately do him justice? His whole life has been devoted to the club, so much so that he can be found at Pittodrie up to nine o'clock every night. He has been a marvellous support to me throughout my time with Aberdeen and I've yet to hear a bad word about him. To sum up his importance to the club there is the story of the time we were playing the preliminary tie

Time for a drink

against Sion that season and we had to change from our normal strip of red to white top, black shorts and black socks. When we opened up the hamper before the game we found that Teddy had packed the wrong socks and I was none too happy. I was cursing him no end and jokingly suggested to the players he was in for the sack. Quick as a flash wee Gordon Strachan declared that that would be nine jobs available at Pittodrie. That gem from the wee man brought the house down.

As the three of us sat there chatting away Teddy and I were able to reflect on what we had achieved and, more importantly, what the future held. Now we were in the goldfish bowl we knew things would get more difficult and other clubs would be looking at our players. We realised then that the hard job was still ahead of us and that having won that Cup, there was now no way back.

We also discussed the possibility of Archie Knox leaving Pittodrie, just as Pat Stanton had. Archie had now been with us for two years and had already spoken to me a few times about his desire to go back into management on his own — he had been manager of Forfar when I had offered him the job. Like Pat he had a hankering to try it on his own. This was in itself no bad thing, for unless an assistant manager has that kind of ambition he is likely to fall into a complacent attitude that the job is his for life. When Pat Stanton left the club I had been quite happy to continue on my own for a while until the right man appeared. Although I didn't know Archie as well as I had known Pat, he looked to have all the right qualities and after speaking to Jim McLean about him I was assured of at least one thing — no amount of hard work would be enough for Archie. So it proved. He was without doubt managerial

Showing the Cup off from the traditional open-top bus

100

A great reception from the crowds in Union Street

Willie and myself with European Cup-Winners' Cup, a couple of tired men

quality and although we enjoyed a good relationship and he shared in that greatest moment of all at Gothenburg, I was happy for Archie when the Dundee job was offered to him. He has proved to be good value at Dens Park by providing a clean sweep and instilling a pride where before there was only apathy.

A mere ten days after Gothenburg it was back to business in the most serious way — a Scottish Cup Final against Rangers. We travelled to Hampden in good spirits and fully anticipating a victory. I was hoping that we would crown the season with a champagne performance and show everyone how much winning in Gothenburg had done for us as a team. I was to be sorely disappointed and although we won the Cup through an Eric Black goal in extra-time, it was a tired performance and a dreary Final. I reacted badly at the final whistle and criticised my players in a television interview immediately after the match. I was to regret that later when I realised that the emotion and excitement of Gothenburg had finally caught up with the team at Hampden. I apologised to the players next day after breakfast at our hotel but it took some time before I felt any better.

Nevertheless, a great season, and a unique double in many ways. The happiness of that year, though, was tinged with two sadnesses dealt out by fate. One was the death of the young Aberdeen supporter on the night of our greatest triumph. And the other was the premature end to Stuart Kennedy's great footballing career.

Lap of Honour at Pittodrie

Mark McGhee and I meet the 'Boat People' to show them the Cup

I first met Stuart as a young boy at Falkirk when I was player/coach and I knew even then he was going to be a great player. He turned out to be an excellent buy for Aberdeen, a consistently successful player for the club and one who gave me every support as manager from the moment I walked into Pittodrie. Stuart was a dedicated professional who took great pride in himself and who was tremendously popular with the other players. He would even bring in clothes he didn't want and gave them to the young boys in the club and it was always Stuart that they turned to for advice — so much so that the chairman called him 'the counsellor'. If he was a counsellor, though, he was also something of the dressing room lawyer, again in the best possible sense. I always knew if we were discussing bonuses or incentives Stuart would be there with all the facts and figures, ready to speak up on the players' side. With my own history as leader of the Players' Union I obviously respected that.

But Stuart Kennedy could also perform on the park. No opponent ever consistently bettered him. He could handle them all with his great pace and strong defensive qualities. Many people often underestimated Stuart and I feel he was still improving at the age of 29. Stuart had been unlucky with injuries prior to that Belgian incident which ended his career, though. He had had pelvic trouble for some time and the tablets he was taking each day to combat that had a nauseous effect on him. When you consider the type of performances Stuart was regularly putting in for the club under that kind of pressure it is all the more commendable. But for those injuries who knows what level he would have reached in the game? Certainly he was one of the cleanest players in the game and for a defender to have only been booked once in his whole career is some achievement. It was a tragedy that football — and Aberdeen — lost Stuart so early.

At least he was able to share in our European success of that season for although he didn't play again after the second Waterschei game we put him on the bench for the Final and it was a great satisfaction for him to pick up his winners' medal.

I'm delighted to see that he's now channelled some of that infectious enthusiasm of his into regular support for the team. He'll always be welcome at Pittodrie.

PREMIER DIVISION CHAMPIONSHIP

	P	W	L	D	F	A	Pts
DUNDEE UNITED	36	24	4	8	90	35	56
CELTIC	36	25	6	5	90	36	55
ABERDEEN	36	25	6	5	76	24	55
RANGERS	36	13	11	12	52	41	38
ST MIRREN	36	11	13	12	47	51	34
DUNDEE	36	9	16	11	42	53	29
HIBERNIAN	36	7	14	15	35	51	29
MOTHERWELL	36	11	20	5	39	73	27
MORTON	36	6	22	8	30	74	20
KILMARNOCK	36	3	22	11	28	91	17

SCOTTISH CUP

Third Round	Hibs	Away	W	4-1	
Fourth Round	Dundee	Home	W	1-0	
Fifth Round	Partick Thistle	Away	W	2-1	
Semi-final	Celtic	Hampden	W	1-0	
Final	Rangers	Hampden	W	2-1	AET

LEAGUE CUP

Qual. Sect.	Morton	Away	D	2-2	
	Dundee	Home	D	3-3	
	Morton	Home	W	3-0	
	Dumbarton	Home	W	3-0	
	Dundee	Away	W	5-1	
	Dumbarton	Away	W	2-1	
Q-final 1st leg	Dundee United	Home	L	1-3	
2nd leg	Dundee United	Away	L	0-1	

EUROPEAN CUP-WINNERS' CUP

Prelim 1st leg	Sion	Home	W	7-0	
2nd leg	Sion	Away	W	4-1	11-1
1st R 1st leg	Dinamo Tirane	Home	W	1-0	
2nd leg	Dinamo Tirane	Away	D	0-0	1-0
2nd R 1st leg	Lech Poznan	Home	W	2-0	
2nd leg	Lech Poznan	Away	W	1-0	3-0
3rd R 1st leg	Bayern Munich	Away	D	0-0	
2nd leg	Bayern Munich	Home	W	3-2	3-2
S-final 1st leg	Waterschei	Home	W	5-1	
2nd leg	Waterschei	Away	L	0-1	5-2
Final	Real Madrid	Gothenburg	W	2-1	AET

Top Scorer: Mark McGhee 22

Chapter Six
1983-84: Double and Treble

HAVING WON the European Cup-Winners' Cup and the Scottish Cup double, the first time the club had ever won a double in major honours, I was looking forward to the new season. With the exception of signing Billy Stark and selling Andy Watson, we had the same pool of players. I felt that if we retained the same hunger there was little that could stop us from getting even better.

We decided to go over to West Germany for a series of pre-season friendly matches but to be honest it turned out to be a long and tedious sojourn. We played a total of eight games in hot and humid conditions and I sympathised with the players, for although a tour like that helps build preparation and fitness, it was an energy-sapping excercise in which we encountered one or two setbacks. At the end of the day, though, it brought the players back down to earth. They realised that all the praise and glory that had surrounded Gothenburg was now forgotten. Things were definitely back to normal.

When we came back from Germany we played a series of friendlies against English opposition. After losing 1-0 to Arsenal we travelled down to Ipswich to play in a testimonial match for George Burley, just as Ipswich had provided the opposition for Drew Jarvie's testimonial at Pittodrie. The Cobbold family who largely own the Ipswich football club are renowned for their generosity and hospitality to visitors and this occasion was no exception. Their generosity did not extend as far as the football pitch, however, and we took a bit of a thrashing, losing 3-0. These bad results soon began to prey on my mind and I considered dropping one or two players. I reasoned, though, that pre-season friendlies are one matter and real competitive games are another, that some of the players were holding back a bit waiting for the season proper to begin. At any rate our next and last friendly match, against Manchester United for Martin Buchan's testimonial, was more encouraging. Trailing 2-0 at half-time, we ended up level through two Peter Weir goals.

At least at the end of the pre-season preparation we were satisfied

John Hewitt scores against Dundee

with our fitness. Although we had shown some form in the game against Manchester United we knew that the real gauge would be our performances in the League. On a hot, sunny 20 August we made a good start to that League programme with a 3-0 victory over Dundee in front of a large crowd. No sooner had we started the League, of course, than the League Cup competition interrupted.

I have some reservations about the League Cup competition — and not just because Aberdeen never won it in my first seven years! The Scottish League Cup has changed format so often that I think it disillusions and confuses supporters and frustrates players. In season 1983-84 it confused everyone no end. In that season we started our League Cup campaign on 24 August 1983, and finished our interest in the competition on 10 March 1984. Supporters tend to lose contact with and interest in the tournament over that kind of extended period. We started off that season's competition fairly well, however, turning in an excellent performance against Raith Rovers at Pittodrie on a lovely Wednesday night. It was one of those games that could be set to music, with Eric Black scoring four times and Billy Stark notching up a hat-trick — an impressive start for Starkie.

Our League form, though, was reasonable rather than brilliant. I had expected more from the players and matters came to a head after a

Martin Buchan's testimonial game against Manchester United

stuttering performance down at Motherwell just prior to our first-leg European match against Akranes in Iceland. In a match notable largely for Aberdeen's missed chances we were leading Motherwell through a solitary McGhee goal, when we should have been three or four up, until later in the game. As so often happens, we paid dearly for our errors and Motherwell scrambled a 1-1 draw by scoring with a few minutes of the game to go. It was time to give a few players a warning that I would not accept that standard.

We travelled to Iceland with our tails between our legs after that Motherwell performance but we were nonetheless confident that the tie against Akranes should be a relatively easy one to see us into the second round of the European Cup-Winners' Cup, a trophy which has never been won by the same team twice in a row. There was a target for us to aim at. What a shock we got. I had left out Peter Weir, who had not been playing very well, as well as Gordon Strachan, who had a niggling injury, and Eric Black, who had a recurrence of a back injury. After a really tough match we were lucky to emerge winners by 2-1 through two Mark McGhee goals. Akranes even missed a penalty in the second-half. It was a lesson for us: to have success in the game, we had to retain our hunger, we had to want to win matches. It was maybe one of the better things to happen to us in that period. We realised we had to try harder.

Our League form continued to be slightly erratic, although we did come back from Iceland to beat Rangers in a fine performance at Ibrox. It was one of those games which showed how brittle the Ibrox supporters could be. While the score was 0-0, the Rangers support were in full song, but as soon as we opened the scoring they started to desert the terracings. It was then that the first really volatile reaction to John Greig as manager was heard and I felt for the man that day. He took a lot of abuse from the terracings and there were even delegations outside the ground. That kind of behaviour is hard on a manager. Nor were the cat-calls based on any realistic premise, for it was not as if Rangers were losing to a smaller second-rate team. Aberdeen had just won the European Cup-Winners' Cup and we had eight internationals in our team. From our point of view we were expecting to win and the demonstrations were rather strange.

After that good result, though, we lost to Dundee United at home. We were down 2-0 midway through the first-half but fluffed a great chance to get back into the game early in the second-half when McMaster missed a penalty kick, and although Strachan converted another penalty later in the game it was too late. It was a disappointing match for Aberdeen and we realised we still lacked consistency. In the

League Cup, meanwhile, we disposed of Meadowbank, St Johnstone and Dundee to take us through to the semi-finals against Celtic, scheduled to be played some time away yet, in February and March.

Eventually, too, we went through to the next round in the European Cup-Winners' Cup by drawing 1-1 with Akranes at Pittodrie on a dirty, wild night that probably resembled Icelandic rather than Scottish weather. The Icelanders, though, battled as if their lives depended on the match and frankly we were delighted to get through 3-2 on aggregate even although we didn't win at home.

In the League we began to make some progress. After losing to Dundee United we realised that if we wanted to win the Championship we'd have to start showing more consistency and it had to start soon. Our next match was against Hearts at Tynecastle on

Mark McGhee beats Paul McStay and Roy Aitken of Celtic

1 October and they had been off to a flyer, coming straight up from the First Division and winning their first five matches of the season. Hearts were top of the League and we were sitting in sixth position. It was a crucial game at a crucial time and even though Hearts would not have been expected to lift the Championship at the end of the season we did not relish the prospect of being six points behind them at the end of the game. A marvellous crowd of over 18,000 turned out at Tynecastle for the match on a sunny day, and among 'them was a sizeable Aberdeen support. We had to show true Aberdeen grit and determination to see off a young and vicious Hearts side and we ended up winners through two Peter Weir goals, the second from a particularly well-executed free kick. That result knocked Hearts down a little and pulled ourselves up a few places in the League.

However, we still lacked consistency. Although we beat St Mirren 5-0 the following week, we then stuttered against Hibs at Easter Road. We were coasting with a 1-0 lead through a Doug Rougvie goal in the first-half and I felt that with all our experience we should have been able to consolidate our lead and go on to win — especially as Hibs had been having a bad season so far. But in the second-half Willie Irvine scored two late goals to clinch the game for Hibs and leave me asking questions about some of my players. It was bad enough losing to Hibs but it was also the worst type of preparation we could have for the following Wednesday when we were due to play Beveren in the second round of the European Cup-Winners' Cup.

Now Beveren were at that stage six points clear at the top of the Belgian League. They were a very competent, well-organised side who played a fairly fluid 4-4-2 and 4-2-4 system. I had sent Archie Knox over to see them and the information that he had brought back was that they were a very tight pack. I knew it was going to be a difficult tie. But now, in the light of our defeat by Hibs, was no time for analysing or examining the players. On the Monday I called one of the crisis meetings we have from time to time and a few things were put firmly and bluntly to the players. I told them frankly that the honeymoon was over and the success of last year was history. I wanted to know what they were going to achieve next and whether their hunger for success had disappeared, whether I would have to go out and look for new players who would have that hunger.

We went to Belgium and earned a creditable 0-0 draw. Beveren started the match well but as the game went on I started to see some grit and determination about our performance. Mark McGhee began to show a lot of his old aggression up front and the fact that he took a lot of abuse in that game made it all the more satisfying to see his aggression returning. Gordon Strachan had been out through injury at that time but I brought him on late in the game as a substitute and it was a tonic to see him back in a match. Straight after that match we came back to meet Celtic in a League match at Pittodrie where we turned in one of our better performances to win convincingly by 3-1. Things were looking up.

Sometimes you have to take a step back to go forward and I feel that was what happened in the case of one or two of our indifferent League displays and certainly our defeat by Hibs. That set us off on a run of twenty-seven games without defeat — exactly the type of consistency required to win the Premier League. The fact that we had not won the League since 1980 but still had basically the same players in our pool was seen as an indictment on the players themselves and they responded well. More important, though, was the manner in which we were winning. I had suffered watching our play because although we were usually the superior team we often allowed the opposition to hang in there instead of killing them off with a few goals. Now there was an improvement in our goalscoring rate and we were turning in some good performances, beating Dundee 3-0 at Dens, St Johnstone 5-0 with a John Hewitt hat-trick, and Rangers 3-0 at Pittodrie in Jock Wallace's first game as manager. That run was very satisfying and the players were beginning to show a consistency that was bringing the team to a peak.

All great things come to an end some time, however, and for us the end came a great many miles away, in front of only a few of our own supporters — in Hungary against Ujpest Dosza. We turned in a particularly inept performance in a match which we could have won but for two of the worst attempts at goalscoring I have ever witnessed. Having taken the temper out of the Hungarians in the first-half, I could hardly believe the chances we missed in the second. The players concerned — Strachan and McGhee — will not thank me for naming them: they certainly won't forget that night and nor will the supporters who watched the TV highlights. McGhee in fact missed from a yard out with the goalkeeper lying in the back of the net. Anyway, having lost 2-0 to such an ordinary team obviously was going to put great pressure on us to chase the game at our own ground. After the match I went straight to my room and wasn't seen again that evening. I was totally disillusioned and disgusted by our performance. Fortunately we did manage to recover at Pittodrie although we had to go to extra-time to do it. Fittingly, Mark McGhee made amends with a first-class performance in which he scored a first-class hat-trick — only his second hat-trick with the club.

The good run had come to an end though, as was emphasised by our exit from the League Cup at the hands of Celtic. We still had a healthy lead in the League, though there too Celtic were chasing us and we had to return to Parkhead a few weeks after our semi-final League Cup defeat. Once again we had a disappointing game and lost 1-0 — the first time during my management at Pittodrie that Celtic had beaten us twice in a row on their own ground. It was particularly hard to accept because we had grown up expecting to win at Parkhead all the time. We usually enjoyed going there but, believe me, when you lose two games in a row it is no longer enjoyment.

From there, though, our performances picked up considerably and the highlight was probably our magnificent display against Dundee United on a fine Wednesday night at Pittodrie when we beat them 5-1. To be fair, the result could have been 10-7. Both teams had some marvellous chances and great strikes at goal but Jim Leighton had one of those games that only he can have while at the other end Hamish McAlpine was performing all sorts of acrobatics. In fact it was a magnificent advert for football and it left the League title within our grasp. I felt that there was no way that we would let it slip now but just to make sure we kept the accelerator down and the next time we lost was after the League was finally won.

Meanwhile we still had the semi-final of the European Cup-Winners' Cup to contend with. The four teams left were Manchester United, Juventus, Porto and Aberdeen. We drew Porto and Willie Garner and I went over to Portugal to have a look at them. I knew then that this would be an extremely difficult task and when I came back I told the players that I had just seen one of the best teams around. They were a marvellous side with mostly small players but they were quick and agile, with good vision, control and energy. Their midfield consisted of international players — Frasco, Vacacco and Souza — and I pointed out clearly the importance of Vacacco.

We prepared as well as we could — in fact as well as we ever had — before going across to play them on their ground for the first leg. Once again we had some injury problems. Peter Weir was out and Mark McGhee and Gordon Strachan were both returning to the team after injury. I took a gamble by also playing Doug Bell who had not had a game since coming back from injury — unfortunately the gamble did not come off. There was a lack of sharpness about our play that night and we had no complaints about losing 1-0, particularly after the first-half when we could have been two or three goals down.

We felt we were still in with a marvellous chance of getting to the Final for the second year in succession. In fact as I was preparing for

Stewart McKimmie against Porto

the second leg I was also preparing for the possibility of meeting either Manchester United or Juventus in Basle. On the night of our match, though, a haar drifted in from the North East and shrouded the ground. There was an eerie, unreal atmosphere and we just didn't get to grips with their midfield. Again I was prepared to take a gamble by putting Peter Weir, who had been out injured for so long, on the substitutes' bench. My thoughts were that if things were going so badly

115

for us or if I needed to go for goals I would bring on Peter in the hope that he would get in a decisive cross for us. I also planned to bring on my other substitute, Billy Stark, to chase for a goal from the other side of the park but unfortunately Stewart McKimmie picked up an injury in the second-half and I had to scrap that idea. With five or six minutes to go Porto raced up the park and their little outside-left, Costa, beat a couple of players before scoring a good goal. We were out of the cup.

Over in Italy Stuart Kennedy, whom I had sent out to compile a report on the second-leg match between Juventus and Manchester United was absolutely flabbergasted for he was engrossed in putting his report together and picking out all the salient points when a Juventus man came up to inform him that Aberdeen were out, having lost 1-0. Meanwhile, at Pittodrie all we could do was wish the Porto team well. The scene in their dressing room was unbelievable. All their staff and it seemed like all their supporters too were in there dancing around. Memories of Gothenburg came drifting back.

While the most important part of the season was the European competition, we were also making progress in the Scottish Cup, although we did get a fright from Kilmarnock at Pittodrie. We were coasting 1-0 with a Peter Weir goal when they stole up the park and scored with the very last kick of the ball. We won 3-1 in the replay at Rugby Park three days later when Gordon Strachan scored one of his special goals after exchanging two or three one-touch passes with other players. Willie Miller then scored from a Peter Weir cross and I felt safe enough to substitute Ian Porteous for Strachan who was having hamstring problems. The second-half was nothing if not a real cup tie. Kilmarnock scored with about twenty minutes to go but from there on we bombarded their goal until a Peter Weir goal put the game beyond doubt.

We played Clyde in the next round and won fairly easily with Ian Angus and Neale Cooper grabbing the goals that took us into the quarter finals to meet Dundee United, our great East Coast rivals. This was to be a two-leg tie without many goals. The Pittodrie game ended up 0-0, although I felt we should have won, and when we went down to Tannadice and scored early in the match through Mark McGhee we were on our way to beating Dundee United in a cup tie for the first time since I took over as manager. We next met their city rivals, Dundee, in the semi-final at Tynecastle when we came back from playing Porto in the first leg. We had a few injuries and Mark McGhee, Stewart McKimmie and Peter Weir were all out but we got through 2-0 with goals from Ian Porteous and Gordon Strachan. Although we were never in any danger, it was always a bit of a battle and it was obvious that Archie Knox had already improved the Dundee team considerably.

We clinched the Premier League title on 2 May at Tynecastle. Perhaps surprisingly our supporters did not attend that match in any great numbers, mainly because we were already so many points ahead of Celtic and they presumed our winning of the Championship to be inevitable. Only 2,000 or 3,000 came down to Edinburgh for the match, in contrast to our League-clinching victory at Easter Road four years before. But winning the title when there were still five League games to be played allowed us to take the foot off the pedal a bit and to rest players here and there in preparation for the Cup Final on 19 May.

By that date we were buzzing and ready to go. The great thing was that all the players were fit, including Peter Weir, and every one of them was keen to play in the Final against Celtic in this, our 76th game of the season. The fact that Celtic were to be our opponents gave the game that extra edge. We had already beaten one half of the Old Firm, Rangers, in the previous two Finals and it would be more than satisfying to complete the double against the other half. We were mindful too that our elimination from the League Cup that year was at the hands of the Parkhead team.

In the lead up to the Saturday we carried out our normal training schedule and went up to Cruden Bay on the Wednesday to give the players training and some relaxation through golf, and also to get them away from the limelight. Our team for the day itself was our strongest and the only gamble I took was in leaving John Hewitt, who had not been playing well, off the substitutes' bench. Instead I opted for two midfielders as substitutes, Billy Stark and Dougie Bell, both of whom were starting to show good form and had the right big match temperament. If one of our strikers were injured Billy Stark could also play in a withdrawn striker position.

We started the game exceptionally well and gave notice right away that we meant to win. We were in the lead with an Eric Black goal and cruising confidently when, with half an hour gone, one of those incidents which mars a game took place. Mark McGhee was well clear with only Roy Aitken to beat when Roy brought him down in a totally unceremonious fashion. The big Celtic player was quite rightly ordered off but by half-time I was wishing the incident had never taken place. Playing against ten men is sometimes the worst thing that can happen to a team and that proved to be the case for Aberdeen on the day.

In the second-half we seemed to go into a lower gear and found it difficult to get back up. It was a nightmare. Celtic dominated the half and very much deserved the equaliser from Paul McStay to take the game into extra-time. I was desperate for the whistle to blow for the first ninety minutes, to get talking to the players and to get them playing like the Aberdeen we knew.

In extra-time we played more like ourselves. Celtic had had their chance and now their players' legs were being drained of energy. Billy Stark and Dougie Bell brought a freshness to our team and the tactical change of putting Neale Cooper up against Davie Provan, who had been giving Rougvie such an uncomfortable second-half, worked well. From there on there was no way back for the Parkhead team. Dougie Bell had a marvellous shot which hit the post. The ball came back for Gordon Strachan who crossed for Mark McGhee to score his last goal for Aberdeen Football Club. The Scottish Cup was ours for the third year in a row.

Team with League & Cup Double
Cowan, Weir, Bell, Angus, McDougall and Falconer.
McQueen, Cooper, Leighton, McIntyre, Gunn, Mitchell and Stark.
Porteous, Hewitt, Black, Miller, McLeish, Simpson, McMaster and McKimmie.

PREMIER DIVISION CHAMPIONSHIP

	P	W	L	D	F	A	Pts
ABERDEEN	36	25	4	7	78	21	57
CELTIC	36	21	7	8	80	41	50
DUNDEE UNITED	36	18	7	11	67	39	47
RANGERS	36	15	9	12	53	41	42
HEARTS	36	10	10	16	38	47	36
ST MIRREN	36	9	13	14	55	59	32
HIBERNIAN	36	12	17	7	45	55	31
DUNDEE	36	11	20	5	50	74	27
ST JOHNSTONE	36	10	23	3	36	81	23
MOTHERWELL	36	4	25	7	31	75	15

SCOTTISH CUP

Third Round	Kilmarnock	Home	D	1-1	
Replay	Kilmarnock	Away	W	3-1	
Fourth Round	Clyde	Away	W	2-0	
Fifth Round	Dundee United	Home	D	0-0	
Replay	Dundee United	Away	W	1-0	
Semi-final	Dundee	Tynecastle	W	2-0	
Final	Celtic	Hampden	W	2-1	AET

LEAGUE CUP

2nd R 1st leg	Raith Rovers	Home	W	9-0
2nd leg	Raith Rovers	Away	W	3-0
Qual. Sect.	Meadowbank	Home	W	4-0
	St Johnstone	Away	W	1-0
	Dundee	Home	D	0-0
	St Johnstone	Home	W	1-0
	Meadowbank	Away	W	3-1
	Dundee	Away	W	2-1
S-final 1st leg	Celtic	Home	D	0-0
2nd leg	Celtic	Away	L	0-1

EUROPEAN CUP-WINNERS' CUP

1st R 1st leg	IA Akranes	Away	W	1-2	
2nd leg	IA Akranes	Home	D	1-1	3-2
2nd R 1st leg	SK Beveren	Away	D	0-0	
2nd leg	SK Beveren	Home	W	4-1	4-1
3rd R 1st leg	Ujpest Dosza	Away	L	0-2	
2nd leg	Ujpest Dosza AET	Home	W	3-0	3-2
S-final 1st leg	Porto	Away	L	0-1	
2nd leg	Porto	Home	L	0-1	0-2

Top Scorer: Mark McGhee 18

Chapter Seven
1984-85: Champions By A Record

WITHIN A relatively short space of time after achieving our second major double in two years, there were important changes at Pittodrie. Unlike the previous year we now had to confront the problems of players opting to take up their freedom of contract. Before the season started Strachan, McGhee and Rougvie had all gone while Frank McDougall and Tommy McQueen had arrived at Pittodrie, from St Mirren and Clyde respectively.

To prepare for the 1984-85 season we had already agreed to go back to Germany, but to a different area and to play against different opposition. We stayed at an old monastery converted into a hotel up in the hills about seven miles away from Koblenz and trained at the stadium which has become so famous for its international athletics meetings. The players loved the area but the great problem was the distance from our base that we had to travel for each match. The agent, Killat, who had organised the tour, was not the most popular man with us anyway as he had also acted on Cologne's behalf in the Gordon Strachan transfer saga, but we had agreed to the itinerary beforehand and had to abide by that agreement. Before long, though, the players were referring to the trip as 'Around the World in Eight Days'.

As in the previous pre-season tour of Germany our form was not great but we regarded the fitness preparation as being more important in a way. We knew that we already had a hard season ahead due to the enforced team changes which the transfers had caused. But what really came as the biggest blow of that German trip were injuries to Peter Weir, who was sent home with a recurrence of his foot injury, and to Neale Cooper, who broke his ankle in one of the games. These injuries were to dog us for the rest of the season.

I began to feel that events were piling up on top of me. I had just lost Strachan, McGhee and Rougvie and was already aware that John McMaster could almost be ruled out through injury for another season, when along comes this double blow of losing Cooper and Weir. I was actually beginning to think that maybe I should have taken one of the

Alex McLeish putting in a strong challenge

recent job offers I had received from Rangers and Spurs. My mind was reeling. But one of the great challenges of football management is whether you have the ability to weather the storms, whether you can be patient under pressure. I decided that I had to be as rational as possible in thinking about the season ahead. The early part could be something of a struggle and it might take some time to get the players organised into a way of playing for each other and into a system that suited them, but once we did get some momentum going we could possibly make a real challenge for a fourth successive Scottish Cup win. This had to be our target, the big incentive for everyone at the club. I approached the season with that in mind.

We certainly made a mixed start to my seventh year as manager of the club. We were knocked out of European competition in the very first round against Dynamo Berlin. I remember first hearing of our being drawn to play against the Berlin club while I was on a Mediterranean cruise in the summer. I just said, 'Oh no.' I felt like jumping into the sea in fact! They had won their league competition for seven years in a row and were nobody's pushover. Perhaps I had something of a premonition. In fact we seemed well in control of the first leg at Pittodrie when we were leading 2-0 but Dynamo scored an important goal towards the end. Over in East Berlin the scoreline was reversed, with our goal coming from Ian Angus. We lost the tie in the worst possible way — through a penalty kick decider.

Our exit from the Skol Cup was also early — in the first round against Airdrie. It was one of those crazy nights that can only happen in football. We travelled down to Airdrie without our front three of Weir, McDougall and Black, all of whom were injured, and played Porteous, Cowan and Falconer in their place. It was a hot and humid Wednesday night. We should have been well ahead in the first-half when Airdrie scored two incredible goals to go in at half-time leading by 2-1. The second-half was a complete disaster for us and at the end of the day we could not deny them their victory. Of course I had to contend with Ally McLeod's war dances at the end of the game and that added salt to my wounds. Once again we were out of the League Cup, though I must say I think this knockout format of the competition to be the best yet and worthwhile for supporters and sponsors alike.

However these disappointments were masked by a tremendous run in the League, starting off well with a 3-2 victory over Dundee after being 2-1 down at half-time. Our character really came through in the second-half. The next week we beat St Mirren down at Love Street, which is always difficult ground to get a result from. But the best performance in the early part of the season was at Tannadice on

Willie Miller

the Saturday after our defeat by Airdrie. The greatest test of any Aberdeen player is always how he reacts to adversity. We can be defeated just as any team can but what is important is how the team react to defeats. We are not in the business of losing two games in a row. We came back off that Airdrie defeat to turn in a marvellous performance and beat Dundee United 2-0 with two Eric Black goals.

It might well be that our early elimination from European competition and from the Skol Cup was no bad thing. With the Scottish Cup not due to start till after the New Year, we were able to prepare especially for each League match. Frank McDougall scored his first League goal for the club in our 4-1 victory over Hibs at Pittodrie and thereafter scored eight goals in eight successive games. That is why teams pay good money for top strikers. Frank's consistent scoring level brought him to the attention of the media and other clubs. Everyone began to comment on the transformation of Frank McDougall since coming to Aberdeen but what was really important in that transformation was that Frank had always had that ability. At Pittodrie we gave him the ambition to match his ability, we gave him a platform to work from with good players around him and we made him adhere to certain disciplines. Ironically, however, Frank missed a glorious chance against Rangers when he was past the keeper and hit the post, and that 0-0 draw was our first minor setback in the League.

Our run resumed with good victories against Dumbarton and Hearts and it was not until we met Celtic at Parkhead that we suffered our first League defeat of the season. In fact in the past few seasons Celtic have proved more difficult than they have ever been against us. That particular defeat at Parkhead was the third time in a row they had beaten us there. I felt sympathy for our players, though. They had played well, especially in the second-half when Frank McDougall scored a brilliant equalising goal. Then Billy Stark missed a penalty kick towards the end of the game. It proved fatal because David Provan hit one of his magnificent free kicks and we were beaten.

After that defeat at Celtic Park we went seven games in a row without dropping a point and with Frank McDougall scoring in every game. These were the kind of statistics and goalscoring rates that any team ambitious to win the League could do with. There was growing confidence and enthusiasm about the club because of this winning sequence. The McDougall/Stark combination was also proving to be a big success and it was to be calculated at the end of that season that there were only five occasions when they were both in the team that at least one of them did not score. At that point, at any rate, our eighth game of the run was looming — against Celtic at Pittodrie.

Now the Parkhead team was being billed as the new Celtic, the best Celtic team since 1967, and there was much to substantiate that claim. One singular stroke of managerial brilliance was their signing of Maurice Johnston from Watford. He was a player with a goalscoring record and his return to Scotland heralded a new era for the Glasgow team. It was a marvellous build up to the Pittodrie match with us having gone our seven victories in a row, top of the League and four points in front of Celtic. The newspapers gave the game great exposure. Even I was bubbling with excitement about the prospect of the game and we worked hard on certain players in preparation for the game. I felt the team was ready for this test.

We turned on one of our best performances for a long time and hammered Celtic 4-2. One of their goals came from a penalty and in fact in the four times we played them that season they scored through three penalty kicks. Anyway, that performance on 8 December 1984 was really great. We did not have a weakness in our team and our enthusiasm and hunger to win was bigger than theirs. Two goals from Eric Black, one from Frank McDougall and a Stewart McKimmie hit which was deflected into the net gave us the cushion we needed — we were six points clear of Celtic in the League and we were still only at the beginning of December.

Any comfort we felt about that, though, was to be short-lived. Some of the younger players in particular seemed to 'peak' in that Celtic game and to forget that we still had half a season to go. The next week we disappointed badly with a terrible home performance which somehow scraped a 0-0 draw with Dundee. Small things started to go wrong. We had niggling injuries throughout this period and also lost Neil Simpson for a while through injury. I rushed Doug Bell back into the team after he had been out for three months with a rib fracture which was compounded when he burst a blood vessel and blood had flooded into his lungs. It had been a serious time for the lad but I was having midfield problems and needed his services. Next we lost to Dundee United through a set-piece move from which Richard Gough scored but followed that up by a creditable draw in a titanic struggle at Love Street when a great Frank McDougall goal brought us back from behind. On New Year's Day we lost to Dundee United once more, with Richard Gough scoring against us again. Out of four games, then, we had salvaged only two points. Our six-point lead over Celtic had quickly diminished, though Celtic also lost to Dundee United in the same period and that kept us to the fore — just.

We were once more on trial in the face of adversity. A mixture of good fortune and the eventual rediscovery of our form saw us through.

We beat Hibs on a cold January afternoon when all the other Premier League matches were postponed through bad weather and although that meant that Celtic now had a game in hand it also meant, more importantly, that we had another two points. Celtic didn't play for the next two weeks either and we managed to go well ahead with victories over Morton, 5-0, and Rangers, 5-1. Ironically, for once the weather in the North East was the best in Scotland and that seemed to bode well for our form.

Against Rangers, when Frank McDougall scored a hat-trick and the other goals came from Eric Black and a Tommy McQueen penalty, it was an annihilation. We were really rampant. The touch and imagination were there. The only black cloud on the day was an unsavoury incident involving McKimmie and the Rangers left-back Dawson. Ally Dawson is in fact known for his bad reaction to strong tackles and I still feel that it was his retaliation to a tackle by Stewart McKimmie that led to McKimmie being shown the red card in that game. In fact the same thing happened previously at Ibrox when Eric Black and Dawson were both given their marching orders. In both cases I was convinced that our players were more sinned against than sinning. I really sympathised with young Stewart that day. At half-time he sat down and almost wept, thinking that he'd let us down. Nonetheless we went on to win 5-1 with the ten men we had left.

If our form in the League was improving, though, our form in the Scottish Cup was little short of erratic. We started well against Alloa in January, winning 5-0, then struggled to a 5-2 victory against Raith Rovers at Kirkcaldy. It was there that our Cup problems really started for Frank McDougall, who scored two good goals that day, was taken off in the second-half with a groin injury which was to keep him niggled and in and out of the team almost to the end of the season. I am convinced that Frank's injury that day cost us dearly and I feel that if we had been able to call on McDougall and Peter Weir with any level of consistency in the Cup competition we would have gone through to the Final. In fact Peter Weir came back into the team for a grand total of fifteen games that year but he was only just regaining his fitness when there was a recurrence of his foot injury. We decided to have the foot operated on in March 1985 in an attempt to solve the problem finally.

We bumbled through the quarter finals eventually after a replay against Hearts at Pittodrie when Billy Stark scored the only goal and big Roddy McDonald was sent off for a foul on Eric Black. In the semi-finals we were again drawn against our great rivals Dundee United and this one also went to a replay after a 0-0 draw at Tynecastle. The replay was scheduled for the same venue despite the fact that there was a rail strike on and extensive repairs were taking place at the Forth Road Bridge. In front of a small crowd in Edinburgh we lost our chance of winning four Scottish Cups in a row, going down 2-1 on the night. As in most 'New Firm' matches there was more than a hint of controversy. There is no doubt in my mind, nor in the minds of any of the spectators there that night, that Maurice Malpas handled the ball in his own penalty area late in the game. The referee seemed to be the only person on the park who didn't see it.

The result, though, did not stop me wishing Jim McLean and Dundee United all good luck in the Final that year. If they had won it would have been another great boost for football in the North East and we supported them just as we would have been given their support in a similar situation. The two clubs, after all, have done so much together for Scottish football in combatting the consistent dominance of the Old Firm. Now, to win something in Scotland you have to beat Aberdeen and Dundee United. On sheer ability, I felt that they would beat Celtic in the Scottish Cup Final. Unfortunately, though, their 'Hampden jinx' seemed to stay with them.

Funnily enough, after struggling through against Hearts in the quarter finals, our League form again picked up dramatically. Immediately after the Hearts game we trounced Dundee 4-0 at Dens Park with Stark grabbing two goals and Black and Simpson completing the rout. Another great away victory followed when we trounced Hibs 5-0 in Edinburgh in a game that included an Eric Black hat-trick. I began to feel sure that if we could win our next two matches — against Dundee United at Pittodrie and against Rangers at Ibrox — we would win the League.

For the United match, again we were the only teams playing in the Premier League on a wet day at a very boggy Pittodrie pitch. Goals from Stark and Cowan, and two from John Hewitt saw us through in a marvellous 4-2 victory. We therefore travelled down to Ibrox in a confident mood, with the players knowing exactly what was at stake. Although we were 2-0 up by half-time through goals by Steve Cowan and Eric Black, a bit of slackness in the second-half allowed Robert Prytz to score and for the last fifteen minutes of the match it was simply a question of hanging on in. Our defenders certainly earned their corn that day — particularly Jim Leighton with two late saves — but hang on in we did.

Mathematically we could still be overtaken in the League but I knew the rest of the season would be a formality. A 4-0 home victory against Dumbarton set us up for our next match at Pittodrie on 27

The Reserve side get into the Trophy winning habit

April against Celtic in a game which many believed to be the real title clincher. A fairly soft penalty put Celtic in the lead that day but it was fitting that our recovery should be sparked off by a Willie Miller goal just before half-time. The example Miller provided that day was the

Joy in the dressing room after the draw with Celtic makes it our Championship

most impressive part of our performance. At any club there are players who will exert a tremendous influence on the others and at Aberdeen I think we are exceptionally fortunate in having three such obviously influential individuals controlling our defence — Miller, McLeish and Leighton deserve every praise that is heaped upon them. At any rate, a 1-1 draw with Celtic was a satisfactory result for us. Our last two games, both victories, against Hearts and Morton, were notable mostly for the fact that Frank McDougall returned to the team with a bang, scoring a hat-trick against the Edinburgh club and one at Greenock.

By the end of the season we had beaten the best ever points total of one season and also scored more goals in one season than the previous best. Taking 59 points from 36 matches in one season was a remarkable achievement in anyone's eyes, so much so that the young team of season 1984-85 will rank alongside the team that won in Gothenburg in 1983.

PREMIER DIVISION CHAMPIONSHIP

	P	W	L	D	F	A	Pts
ABERDEEN	36	27	4	5	89	26	59
CELTIC	36	22	6	8	77	30	52
DUNDEE UNITED	36	20	9	7	67	33	47
RANGERS	36	13	11	12	47	38	38
ST MIRREN	36	17	15	4	51	56	38
DUNDEE	36	15	14	7	48	50	37
HEARTS	36	13	18	5	47	64	31
HIBERNIAN	36	10	19	7	38	61	27
DUMBARTON	36	6	23	7	29	64	19
MORTON	36	5	29	2	29	100	12

SCOTTISH CUP

Third Round	Alloa	Away	W	5-0
Fourth Round	Raith Rovers	Away	W	2-1
Fifth Round	Hearts	Away	D	1-1
Replay	Hearts	Home	W	1-0
Semi-final	Dundee United	Tynecastle	D	0-0
Replay	Dundee United	Tynecastle	L	1-2

LEAGUE CUP

2nd R	Airdrie	Away	L	1-3

EUROPEAN CUP

1st R 1st leg	Dynamo Berlin	Home	W	2-1	
2nd leg	Dynamo Berlin	Away	L	1-2	3-3

Knocked out on Penalties After Extra Time.

Top Scorer: Frank McDougall 22

TOP SCORERS IN SEVEN YEARS

McGHEE	103	COWAN	13
STRACHAN	90	COOPER (NEALE)	10
HEWITT	56	ANGUS	9
BLACK	54	KENNEDY	8
ARCHIBALD	40	DAVIDSON	8
HARPER	39	SULLIVAN	8
JARVIE	35	PORTEOUS	8
STARK	33	HARROW	6
WEIR	30	FALCONER	5
SIMPSON	28	HAMILTON	4
McDOUGALL	25	McKIMMIE	4
SCANLON	25	McQUEEN	4
ROUGVIE	22	COOPER (NEIL)	3
McMASTER	20	FLEMING	2
McLEISH	19	GARNER	2
WATSON	19	MITCHELL	2
McCALL	16	McLELLAND	2
MILLER	15	DE CLERCK	1
BELL	15	OWN GOALS	17

Chapter Eight
Old Firm, New Firm

SCOTTISH FOOTBALL has changed dramatically since the inception of the Premier League in 1975 and though some English managers still labour under the misconception that the game up here is somehow inferior, the competitive edge among the top ten clubs is fiercely evident. Nowhere is this more the case than among the top four teams — the 'Old Firm' of Rangers and Celtic and the 'New Firm' of Aberdeen and Dundee United.

History points quite clearly to the fact that in order to achieve anything in Scottish football you must beat the Old Firm. These two teams have been the dominant force for more than fifty years. Over the past seven years, though, the assumption that one of the Old Firm teams would pick up the honours has been brought into question. Rangers last won the Premier League in 1978, while Celtic's last championship title was in 1982. In the past seven years Celtic have won the Premier League three times, Aberdeen three times and Dundee United once; Celtic have lifted the Scottish Cup twice, Aberdeen three times and Rangers twice; Dundee United have won the League Cup twice, Rangers four times and Celtic once. The turning point really came in 1980 when Aberdeen won the Premier League Championship and Dundee United lifted the League Cup. A new force was evident and is here to stay. I would now suggest that to win anything in Scottish football you have to beat Aberdeen and Dundee United.

The rise of the two North-East teams is good for that part of the country and beneficial to Scottish football as a whole. Jim McLean and I have the same kinds of problems in football, particularly in having to compete against the Old Firm, and now of course having to compete against one another. Although we are great friends, believe me, sometimes it's a love-hate relationship. The intensity at Aberdeen-Dundee United matches is now greater than at an Old Firm game. It has reached the stage now where we need the best referees to handle the matches because of their speed and competitiveness and the tactical awareness of both sets of players. There have been some great battles between the two teams as the years have gone on and if you examine the records at the end of this chapter you will see a slight element of failure on our part in games against Dundee United, particularly in Cup matches. In fact our record against Dundee United in the League Cup is so bad that we have only scored two goals in six matches. In the Scottish Cup our record is even, having played four times, won one, lost one and drawn two, but in the League our record is much better.

Our record against the Old Firm is very good, particularly after my first season at Pittodrie. For example, we have not lost a Scottish Cup tie against Celtic and have only lost one League Cup tie to them. Against Rangers we have lost one League Cup Final, the one in which Doug Rougvie was wrongly sent off. But we've also beaten Rangers twice in the League Cup and twice in the Scottish Cup — both times in the Final after extra-time. In the League we have a good record against both of them. There is no doubt, though, that these matches have helped to develop our players and have encouraged them to rise to the big occasion.

The competition among the four teams is so strong that any one of them looks forward to any of the other three playing against each other, knowing that one of their rivals at least must drop points. Certainly at Aberdeen that kind of thinking encourages us in our own game. In that context it is interesting to look back over the seasons to assess our own performances.

My first season at Pittodrie brought the first success against the Old Firm in the form of our defeat of Celtic in the Scottish Cup. The tie went to a dramatic replay full of incident and controversy at Celtic Park but we won through by 2-1. Unfortunately all our efforts in getting into the Scottish Cup semi-final were in vain for we lost that stage to Hibs. We did, however, make it as far as the League Cup Final where we lost 2-1 to Rangers in the game with the controversial Doug Rougvie and Derek Johnstone incident. No tangible success for the Dons, then, in that first year.

In the next season, 1979-80, we beat Celtic and Rangers twice each over two legs in the League Cup and felt that this was the best chance we had yet had of winning the trophy. We met Dundee United in the Final and lost in the replay, 3-0. Although we lost our first game at Parkhead that season, I still think that the making of the Aberdeen team was when we beat Celtic twice within ten days on their own home ground and in front of their own fanatical supporters. There is no doubt that the Aberdeen players came of age on that day of the second match. Again in that season, we played Rangers seven times, winning one, drawing once and losing once. Unfortunately the one match we did lose to them was the most important one, the semi-final of the Scottish Cup. After having outplayed them for the whole game we lost to a late Derek Johnstone goal. The next week, however, we were back in Glasgow to beat Celtic and confirm our position at the top of the League. All in all, then, a fine season against the Old Firm, particularly our beating Rangers five times — a remarkable achievement by any standards.

1981-82 was the season Dundee United knocked us out of the League Cup despite us having the advantage of winning the first leg at Tannadice through a Peter Weir goal. We were hammered 3-0 in the return leg at Pittodrie. In the League, depite losing 4-1 at Tannadice in the first game of the season, we came back to beat United on their home ground in a New Year match, and a further draw and a victory at home gave us five out of eight points against them that season.

In the Scottish Cup that year we beat Celtic in a really remarkable game at Pittodrie which did as much as any other match to change the fortunes of Aberdeen Football Club. I told the players at the time that although this was a fourth round tie it was going to be the real Cup Final as far as we were concerned. We beat them 1-0 with a John Hewitt goal in a match we had worked hard at tactically beforehand and in which Alex McLeish was outstanding. Our hunger to win the Cup helped us to ignore the fact that Celtic had beaten us 3-1 in a League game at Pittodrie just a few weeks before, when they had been allowed too much room in the middle of the park and Charlie Nicholas really turned it on to show us the form we all know he really has.

We came back with a great League run towards the end of that season but left it just too late. Celtic pipped us by a point. The only success we had that year was in the Scottish Cup where we ran out 4-1 winners in the Final against Rangers. Our League record against Rangers that season was also very good. We beat them 4-0 the week before the Scottish Cup Final, with John Hewitt scoring a first-half hat-trick. There was tremendous excitement at half-time in that game, for being 4-0 up we had a chance of clinching the League if Celtic dropped any points. It wasn't to be and Celtic eventually defeated St Mirren at Celtic Park to clinch the title. Nevertheless we had taken seven points out of eight against Rangers in the League and we had also won the Scottish Cup for the first time since 1970 — all in all, quite a satisfactory season.

The next season, though — 1982-83 — was to be unforgettable. But again Dundee United knocked us out of the League Cup, winning

3-1 at Pittodrie and 1-0 at Tannadice. In the League we lost 2-0 at Tannadice in the opening game of the season and then beat them 5-1 at Pittodrie in October. Gordon Strachan was magnificent that day, scoring the last goal with a marvellous piece of quick thinking when he collected the ball on the left side of the park, dribbled into the box and side-footed the ball wide of Hamish McAlpine and into the net. At New Year we went down to Tannadice and beat them 3-0 in another marvellous performance in which our defence played particularly well. Later in the season they beat us 2-1 at Pittodrie when they were in the middle of a marvellous League run which culminated in them winning the title. United caught us on the hop that day after our midweek second-leg match against Bayern Munich and went on to beat us by one point in winning the League. I'm certain that that result inspired them to their marvellous achievement that year.

We beat Celtic in the semi-final of the Scottish Cup in 1983 in a very hard and physical game in which we had four players injured. In fact two of them, Doug Bell and Stuart Kennedy, both missed the European Cup-Winners' Cup Final because of injuries sustained in that game. In the League we took six points out of eight from Celtic.

That season we shared our League points with Rangers and, believe it or not, Rangers chalked up their first ever Premier League victory at Pittodrie. Our second Pittodrie game against them, though, was a marvellous game which we won 2-0 but which will be memorable for John McDonald's sending off after he had butted Doug Bell. Of course, we also beat Rangers that year in the Scottish Cup Final just after we had lifted our European trophy at Gothenburg and though the Final was something of a flat affair we knew that if we could beat Rangers when we were playing badly, then we had to be a good side.

Season 1983-84 was to bring about more than its share of confrontations between Celtic and Aberdeen. Apart from our normal four League games we also had to face them in a two-leg semi-final in the League Cup and in a Scottish Cup Final. In the League we got off to a great start with a 3-1 victory over them at Pittodrie but an untidy 0-0 draw at Parkhead in our second meeting put an end to a good run of victories for us. The decisive League victory for us against Celtic came in February 1984 in a rather lucky win which gave us a healthy points lead over our rivals at a vital time in the run-in to the end of the season. Celtic's courage that season, though, was not to be denied, and after drawing 0-0 with us at Pittodrie in the first-leg of the League Cup semi-final, they deservedly went through to the Final after defeating us by the only goal of the game at Parkhead. For both ourselves and

Celtic, though, the highlight of the season should have been the Scottish Cup Final in front of a crowd of 58,000 at Hampden. We ended up 2-1 winners but the game was marred by Roy Aitken's sending-off. Ironically, that incident caused *our* play to go to pieces and it took us till extra-time to clinch our third consecutive Scottish Cup.

Against Rangers we took six points out of a possible eight in 1983-84, our best result against them probably being our 3-0 victory over them at Pittodrie in their first game since the return of big Jock Wallace to Ibrox. Meanwhile we were also taking five points out of eight against Dundee United, the highlight of these particular clashes being our 5-1 victory at Pittodrie in a game which was a glorius advert for Premier League football.

Last season, 1984-85, which completed my seven years at Aberdeen, was in all honesty a mixed one in terms of results against our great rivals. Celtic, for instance, had their most successful season against us, taking five points out of eight. Our first encounter ended 2-1 in their favour after a magnificent Davie Provan free kick defeated us. In December we turned the tables with a great performance in a 4-2 victory at Pittodrie, but in our third meeting they again asserted themselves with a 2-0 win in Glasgow. It was a sweet moment then when our final game of the season with them clinched the Championship for Aberdeen with a 1-1 draw.

As in the case of Celtic, Dundee United also took more points off Aberdeen last year than they had done in any season since my arrival at Pittodrie. What was particularly disappointing there, however, was that our games against United tend to be rather tousie affairs in comparison to some of the great games between these teams in the past. Our most important meeting with them was, of course, in the Scottish Cup semi-final, when they beat us 2-1 after a 0-0 draw, thus denying us the unique opportunity of winning the trophy for a record four successive seasons. In the League we shared the points.

Our games against Rangers last season were, in fact, amongst the most satisfactory of our League title successes. We lifted seven points out of eight after twice defeating them 2-1 at Ibrox, drawing at Pittodrie, and then slaughtering them 5-1 at home in our last meeting of the season. That last victory at Pittodrie amounted to Rangers' biggest ever defeat in the Premier League.

All in all, over the past seven years I must say there have been some tremendous battles in New Firm and Old Firm games and for most of the time these games have been good for Scottish football. They often capture the public's imagination and certainly swell attendance figures. Although they tend to be fairly intense affairs, where nothing is given away, I would be less than honest if I didn't say there are many players among all three of our main rivals for whom I have only the greatest respect. Some of them I should probably have signed myself!

Roy Aitken is, to me, the most outstanding player among all our opponents in the Premier League. Many people argue that Danny McGrain is the biggest single influence over Celtic but they underestimate the tremendous inspirational play of Aitken. Although there have been times when I have felt that big Roy has bullied opponents and even tried to referee games he is without doubt a magnificent Celtic player. Having got to know him a little through our mutual involvement with the Scotland team I can also vouch for the fact that you couldn't meet a nicer man.

Other Celtic players who have impressed me over the years obviously include Charlie Nicholas who was a marvel on his day with the Parkhead team and who showed all the class that great players have. Tommy Burns is an elegant, left-footed player who has great composure on the ball and is an asset to any team. Paul McStay's potential is there for all to see and he will, in time, prove his greatness. The great bonus as far as Paul is concerned is his down-to-earth lifestyle. I must confess that one player I should have tried to sign when he was with Partick Thistle is Mo Johnston, while I have always admired Murdo MacLeod, whose appetite and willingness to work has made him a key player in the Celtic set-up.

Rangers have had their share of good individuals over the years and, although not as successful as their great rivals, they can list the likes of Peter McCloy, a great character and a loyal servant to them, and Sandy Jardine, who remained an influence even though his best playing days were behind him. Jim Bett has undoubtedly been the best Rangers player over that seven-year period, so much so that he is now safely in our keep! But John McClelland is the one player Rangers allowed to leave whom I am sure they are still missing. His departure from Ibrox may have been decisive in terms of Rangers' fortunes last season and he is a player I would have loved to have signed for Aberdeen. A sound and quick player, he has abilities which would be a great asset to any team. Many were surprised that money proved a stumbling block for Rangers in re-signing the big defender. Davie Cooper is another who has had his re-signing problems with the Ibrox club but the fact that he has decided to stay is good news for Rangers. He is easily the most influential member of the current side. A classy player with great composure and vision, and a marvellous left foot to match.

Down at Tannadice there have been quite a few excellent players over the years, and none more so than Maurice Malpas. He is a dream of a player, with awareness, balance, intelligence, skill and competitiveness — in essence a truly modern footballer. Richard Gough is another youngster in the same mould who will undoubtedly be a great player. I would say that Gough is, in fact, the biggest influence in the present United team. The two centre-backs, Hegarty and Narey, show great understanding with each other and have been great club servants, while behind them they have one of the great characters of football in Hamish McAlpine, a real rarity in the hectic and tense atmosphere of present day football, but also a real breath of fresh air on the scene. Up front, Paul Sturrock and Eamonn Bannon have been inspirational to Dundee United in their drive towards the honours. When these two play well, United play well. Paul is elusive and alert and shows a fine understanding of the game as well as the ability to turn sharply with the ball to evade opponents. Eamonn shows astounding stamina and is seen to his best in a dead ball situation or when putting over devastatingly accurate crosses after a splendid run down the wing.

Although at times, like any manager, I've been wrapped up totally in the affairs and performances of my own team, my admiration for teams like Dundee United, Celtic and Rangers — and particularly the individual players in these teams that I have mentioned — has never been clouded. It must be a source of even further satisfaction to them to know that they have been responsible for many of my sleepless nights!

ABERDEEN v RANGERS
August 1978 — May 1985

OVERALL

P	W	D	L	F	A
36	20	9	7	59	28

LEAGUE

Home

P	W	D	L	F	A
14	9	4	1	28	8

Away

P	W	D	L	F	A
14	6	5	3	17	13

Total

P	W	D	L	F	A
28	15	9	4	45	21

LEAGUE CUP

Home

P	W	D	L	F	A
2	2	0	0	6	2

Neutral

P	W	D	L	F	A
1	0	0	1	1	2

Away

P	W	D	L	F	A
2	1	0	1	2	1

Total

P	W	D	L	F	A
5	3	0	2	9	5

SCOTTISH CUP

Home

—

Neutral

P	W	D	L	F	A
3	2	0	1	5	2

Away

—

Total

P	W	D	L	F	A
3	2	0	1	5	2

ABERDEEN v CELTIC
August 1978 — May 1985

OVERALL

P	W	D	L	F	A
37	18	9	10	53	38

LEAGUE

Home

P	W	D	L	F	A
14	6	4	4	25	19

Away

P	W	D	L	F	A
14	6	3	5	17	13

Total

P	W	D	L	F	A
28	12	7	9	42	32

LEAGUE CUP

Home

P	W	D	L	F	A
2	1	1	0	3	2

Away

P	W	D	L	F	A
2	1	0	1	1	1

Total

P	W	D	L	F	A
4	2	1	1	4	3

SCOTTISH CUP

Home

P	W	D	L	F	A
2	1	1	0	2	1

Neutral

P	W	D	L	F	A
2	2	0	0	3	1

Away

P	W	D	L	F	A
1	1	0	0	2	1

Total

P	W	D	L	F	A
5	4	1	0	7	3

ABERDEEN v DUNDEE UNITED
August 1978 — May 1985

OVERALL

P	W	D	L	F	A
38	14	11	13	49	46

League

Home							Away					
P	W	D	L	F	A		P	W	D	L	F	A
14	6	3	5	24	19		14	6	5	3	21	15

Total

P	W	D	L	F	A
28	12	8	8	45	34

LEAGUE CUP

Home						Neutral						Away					
P	W	D	L	F	A	P	W	D	L	F	A	P	W	D	L	F	A
2	0	0	2	0	4	2	0	1	1	0	3	2	1	0	1	2	3

Total

P	W	D	L	F	A
6	1	1	4	2	10

SCOTTISH CUP

Home						Neutral						Away					
P	W	D	L	F	A	P	W	D	L	F	A	P	W	D	L	F	A
1	0	1	0	0	0	2	0	1	1	1	2	1	1	0	0	1	0

Total

P	W	D	L	F	A
4	1	2	1	2	2

Chapter Nine
The Club

TO GET THE real image of Aberdeen Football Club you really have to come into the ground the morning after a European tie at Pittodrie, particularly if the team have turned on a good performance the night before. A galaxy of football people from all over Britain who have attended the match and stayed overnight in the city will be in there to express their thanks to Aberdeen Football Club for the friendship and hospitality they have received. The general atmosphere is very low key and down-to-earth with staff and directors mixing in friendly chit-chat with the visitors. It is at such times that the unpretentious and family atmosphere of the club is most visible.

The chairman, Dick Donald, is a former Dons player who has been like a father to me in my seven years with Aberdeen. He above anyone has given the club its down-to-earth image. Despite his own marvellous success as a businessman, he is totally unaffected as a person. He has never changed and that is his secret. His humility is the pervading factor at Pittodrie and the club operates from that base. As chairman his approach is low-key and his attitude is that people are employed to do a certain job or perform a certain function and they should be left to do just that. I have always believed that the most important relationship at any football club is that between manager and chairman and I must say that I've been more than fortunate to develop a close relationship with Dick Donald. I have many fond memories of the man which will never leave me but the one which I will never forget is how he and the other directors at the time, Mr Anderson and the late Mr Forbes, stood by me during the period of my tribunal with St Mirren.

Chris Anderson, a club director, is the man of ideas and vision at Pittodrie and is always looking to improve the club's image and project its presence on to the wider community. He provides a fine balance to the chairman and together they are a great team. Chris Anderson is also a former Aberdeen player and with that sort of background is well aware of the difficulties of running a football team. He has retired

142

Daren Ferguson, learning the trade?

143

from business now and can bring his top-class administrative skills to bear on that side of the club.

The chairman's son, Ian Donald, a former Manchester United player, joined the board as a young man after the death of Mr Forbes. A bright man who obviously follows in his father's footsteps, he has his own opinions which will surely help him in the years ahead. He will become a tremendous asset to the club.

Collectively, as a board, these three men are marvellous for Aberdeen Football Club. They continually reassure me that we are all operating in the same cause, which makes it easy for us to operate with a unity. The fact that we often meet in an informal way over lunch helps to build up the family atmosphere at the club. There is no stuffed shirt atmosphere about the boardroom and in fact very few actual board meetings — a unique set-up in every way. It is a manager's dream to have a board like ours and I'm proud to have worked with them.

The club itself is easily managed because of the continuity of a tight-knit and devoted staff. While the chairman has served the club for 50 years and Chris Anderson has been at Pittodrie over 20 years, my secretary Barbara Cook, who together with Brenda Cranstoun does such a marvellous job of lightening my workload, has been with the club for 18 years. Ian Taggart, the club secretary, has also served for ten years. On the development side Fred Booth and his girls, Lorraine White, Pat Johnson, Peggy Petrie and Ashley Reid run a tight ship and that is one of the club's secrets — no matter our success we have never tried to broaden the personnel by bringing in administrative or public relations managers. Everyone pulls together to create a positive and friendly atmosphere. Jim Bett proved the point when he arrived. He had heard how good a club Aberdeen was but was taken aback by the total friendliness and helpfulness of the staff.

Along the corridor from the offices is Teddy Scott's room. Teddy was a junior player with Sunnybank till 1955 and ever since then has devoted his life to Aberdeen Football Club. Although Teddy is happy to stay in the background, all the players know just how much they owe to this man who has instilled discipline and good habits into them. He knows everything that is happening on the playing side and is down there dealing with the players when I'm caught up in my office or dealing with the directors. Teddy has been my right arm in my seven years at Pittodrie.

There also you will find Willie Garner, my assistant, and David Wylie, the club physiotherapist. Willie, a former player, was asked to come back to Pittodrie to assist me some months after Archie Knox

I must have a problem, talking to Dick Donald

left to manage Dundee. I had come to the conclusion after Archie's departure that one problem I had at the club was in not being able to hold on to my assistant managers long enough. Although Pat Stanton had stayed with the club for two years and Archie Knox for three, no sooner had I begun to get used to them than they were away to pursue their own ambitions — actions, incidentally, which I endorsed wholeheartedly. In choosing Willie I felt that he was young enough to learn and to be patient before he has to decide for himself what his future holds.

David Wylie is the third physio we have had at the club in my time as manager and has proved to be a tremendous asset. He has a great relationship with the players despite the fact that he did not endear himself too well with one William Miller Esq upon his arrival at the club. Just after Dave joined us we went over to Germany for pre-season preparation. At our first game over there Willie questioned why his tie-ups for his socks had not been specially cut to size, a duty which had always been performed religiously and meticulously by our last physio,

145

Roland Arnott. The captain's plea, though, was met by a nonplussed Mr Wylie: 'Who do you think you are? Tommy O'Hara?' That response brought the house down for O'Hara had been an average player with Motherwell when Dave was physio there. Willie, of course, was none too pleased and let the wee man know about it, but his complaints fell on deaf ears. The players carried the joke on and gave Willie a terrible ribbing. At the end of the day David Wylie had made his mark and proved to the lads that he was no soft touch.

Further down the corridor is where you will find Pittodrie's pensioners — old people who have supported Aberdeen all their lives and who are so devoted to the club that they are there every day, cleaning the ground and the seats and getting the pitch ready for the following Saturday. It's a treat to sit with them on a bench at the side of the park and just listen to their banter and their advice on what should be done with the team and whom I should be buying. Two men on whom you can rely to be there are George Perry, who looks after the lads' boots, and John Coutts, who does various odd jobs round the stadium.

On the playing side, one of the most important aspects of the club is discipline. At Pittodrie we believe that a well-disciplined side is a successful side. What I look for is responsible behaviour, whether on the park, in the dressing room, away from the stadium or travelling abroad. I expect players to act in a manner which is a credit to both the club and themselves. I often point out to them that every time they are in view of the public they are being judged. I also firmly believe that self-discipline is a key factor in the realisation of any great sportsman.

When young players arrive at Pittodrie, often straight from school, we are particularly hard on them. From the very first minute we teach them self-discipline to prepare them for public exposure. This can be hard on some of the youngsters for, naturally enough, when they reach a stage of public adulation there is a danger of vanity taking over. We try to teach them to retain a certain humility in the face of success. This training is every bit as important as any technical or tactical knowledge we may teach.

Our discipline record is very good in fact, especially compared to some other clubs. In season 1982-83, the year we won the European Cup-Winners' Cup, for instance, not one player was suspended the whole season and not one player missed a European tie through suspension — a quite remarkable achievement under the modern disciplinary code. I do feel that this aspect should be recognised more, especially in an era where there is so much criticism of the modern players.

It is widely known that I never discuss any form of discipline in public for the simple reason that I don't believe in publicly embarrassing a player or his family. I will not break any confidences with players either past or present. None of them were consistent offenders anyway. But to give an example of monetary loss through indiscretion on the park, I once fined a player £750 for an off-the-ball assault on an opponent. That was a severe punishment, but a justified one in as much as it was a very important game for the club and if the player had been sent off — as he should have been — his actions could have cost us dearly. I had to get the message across that the manner of winning is just as important as the victory itself.

Another time I fined one of our players £500 for his involvement in an unsavoury incident in the dressing room after we had beaten Celtic 1-0 in the Scottish Cup in 1982. Two Celtic players were also involved and just as I was ordering them out of the dressing room Billy

Peter Weir and Teddy Scott

McNeill came along and immediately assumed I was bullying his lads. Inevitably an argument flared up between us but, in fairness to Billy, he later apologised when he heard what had actually happened.

I have also fined players fairly heftily for senseless indiscretions such as dissent on the field. Overall, though, I'm delighted to say that the number of times I have had to act severely to impose discipline in my time at Pittodrie would not be enough to fill a postcard. Discipline, like everything else, reflects the high standards of the club and is achieved at Pittodrie not just by luck, but by design.

Chapter Ten
Balancing the Books

ONE ASPECT OF modern football which fascinates all those in the game is the operation of the transfer market and at the end of the day the transfer merry-go-round can be as important to a manager and to his club's success as picking the right team for a match. As a manager I'm always conscious of the fact that if I spend money to bring a player to Pittodrie — no matter how great or small the amount — then that player must fit in to the club successfully. This line of thought has prevented me from going too wildly into the transfer market. In fact, in my seven years at Aberdeen I have only bought twelve players — hardly excessive in the modern era of freedom of contract. During that period the smallest fee we received was for a young lad, David Thomson, who was desperately homesick and whom we sold to Airdrie for £2,000, while the largest transfer was obviously that of Steve Archibald to Tottenham Hotspur for £800,000.

As soon as I arrived to take up the manager's office at Aberdeen I was met with a transfer request from a player I knew very little about. Ian Gibson was, in fact, threatening to emigrate unless he got the move he so badly wanted. Without hesitation I decided to let him go and he moved to Kilmarnock for £17,500. The deal was carried out by that great character, Tom Lauchlan, the Kilmarnock chairman. Typical of the man he came straight to the point. 'How much do you want?' I said, '£17,500.' 'Is he worth that?' I said, 'I believe so, having spoken to Teddy Scott. I would give regard to whatever he says.' 'Right, the deal is done, son,' he said. No messing about and no arguments. I must say I was overwhelmed by his forthright method and made a mental note of that procedure.

Shortly after that Ally McLeod came to me about Joe Smith. Joe had been a lynchpin for Aberdeen when Ally was in charge at Pittodrie and Ally wanted him to do a similar job for Motherwell. We quickly agreed on a fee of £40,000 and Joe was on his way.

Next on our selling list was Ian Fleming who went to Sheffield Wednesday for £45,000. I considered this a great piece of business on our part as Ian was an average player and, although he was as brave as a lion, he never really proved to me that he wanted to play for the club. It is interesting to see Ian now managing Brechin and doing very well but I must confess he is the last player I would have expected to become a manager. I well remember having to train him on his own in the afternoons as his discipline in training was poor and his influence might have been detrimental to the younger players. Now that he's a manager he might appreciate that it's not an easy job and there may even be a twinge of remorse when he remembers his Aberdeen days. At any rate, I wish him well.

All in all, then, not a bad bit of business for my first season at Pittodrie, with an income in excess of £100,000. The profit, though, was not to lie in the bank for too long. It became obvious that Mark McGhee was available for transfer from Newcastle United who had signed him from Morton for £150,000. As I mentioned, I had tried desperately to get him from Morton when I was manager at St Mirren and was scuppered for a meagre £5,000. I was determined to get him this time.

The McGhee transaction, though, dragged on and on for about three months. The main problem was Newcastle's manager, Bill McGarry. Everytime I spoke to him on the phone there was one drawback or another and he gave me the impression tht he was just not sure whether to sell or not. He wasn't so worried about the drop in fee from what they had paid for McGhee — we had been talking around the £60,000 to £70,000 mark — as he was about whether he might give the player another chance in the first team as he had looked good in training. As you can imagine, it was a frustrating business for us. Pat Stanton and I were by this time working hard to get our chairman to raise the offer, hoping this would finally swing the deal. Eventually the respective directors reached agreement and we paid Newcastle £70,000. It proved to be one of our best moves, for Mark McGhee gave Aberdeen sterling service, scoring 103 goals for the club in five years before being transferred at a profit of £210,000.

Season 1979-80, though notable for our winning the Premier League Championship, saw little coming and going from Pittodrie — but what little it did see resulted in an immense profit. Dom Sullivan went to Celtic for £82,000 and quite frankly I was glad to see him leave Pittodrie for the simple reason that his heart wasn't in the club. Like his friend Ian Fleming his presence at the club was beginning to annoy me. Then, of course, Steve Archibald joined Spurs. Aberdeen really had no chance of keeping Steve once he'd made up his mind to move and with freedom of contract looming it was a sensible and extremely profitable transaction for us to sell him for £800,000.

The next season was a real contrast with us being involved time and time again in the hurly-burly of the transfer world. Bobby Clark's back injury led to us signing Marc de Clerck from Twente Enschede for £26,000. Then, of course, young John Gardiner, the goalkeeper, became unsure of his future and wanted a move. We transferred him to Dundee United for £25,000 and although he never quite managed to oust Hamish McAlpine he did a fair job for the Tannadice men. Jim McLean says he'll never forgive me but I know he's joking. Keeping fringe players happy is undoubtedly the hardest job of all for a manager. On the one hand the club needs a good pool to back up the regular team in the quest for honours, but on the other hand you have to feel sympathy for those members of the squad who are not being given games regularly. If they are really ambitious, how can you keep them?

Around that period we had a few fringe players in exactly that situation. It was with some reluctance that we sold Neil Cooper (not Neale) to Barnsley. Allan Clarke, the Barnsley manager, proved particularly hard to deal with in that instance and actually managed to knock me down from my evaluation of £45,000 to £35,000. His name went into the black book after that! Young Steve Morrison was another player who went at that time, to Dunfermline, though the actual settlement — £5,000 — wasn't paid until Steve had played 35 games with them. This kind of conditional transfer has become more prevalent in recent years as the shortage of cash has hit clubs but in this case we were also delighted to give a helping hand to Pat Stanton, my former assistant who was now in charge of the Fife club. His directors were delighted with that buy although the same could not be said for the next player who moved to Dunfermline from Aberdeen. Doug Considine was a fairly competent defender who never really made the grade at Pittodrie so we agreed a deal to sell him to Dunfermline for £35,000. Unfortunately for them, Doug only played for a short time with them before deciding to retire to start a dry cleaning business in Stonehaven. Remarks about Dunfermline having been taken to the cleaners were in distinctly bad taste!

That season it seemed that there was much more going than coming around Pittodrie but that wasn't necessarily a bad thing. When I arrived there had been a distinct overload of playing staff — 41 to be exact. These transfers helped to reduce that financial burden on the club and it was only really the void created by Archibald's transfer which motivated us to buy.

In this context I have to admit to my only real failure in my dealings in the transfer market for Aberdeen. Andy Harrow, whom I bought from Luton Town for £65,000, did not fulfil my hopes. Although he was technically a good player he lacked the belief I was looking for in Aberdeen players. We eventually sold him to Jock Wallace, who was managing Motherwell at the time, for £40,000. Andy was joined in that transfer, for another £10,000, by another of our fringe players, Andy Dornan. He was certainly not short of the belief that Harrow was lacking but his ability was at times questionable, especially in defence. Nonetheless Andy Dornan was a smashing lad and I was delighted he was given a chance by another Premier League team.

Walker McCall was another player I brought to Pittodrie that season in an attempt to replace Archibald. We paid £25,000 to bring him back from the United States and for that sort of money he was a great buy. He was an extremely nice person and a marvellous finisher on the park, even though he was not a player who could command a place in the team every week. Walker stayed with us for about two years before being transferred to play in Hong Kong for about £3,000.

At the end of season 1980-81, though, we proved to our supporters that we not only sold big but could also spend money. For quite a while I had been trying to get Peter Weir to Pittodrie but was given no joy at all from Jim Clunie, the St Mirren manager at the time, and it was only when he left and Ricky McFarlane took over at Love Street that I was finally able to land him. Weir came to Aberdeen for £220,000 plus Ian Scanlon but the other factor which swung the deal was our promise not to sign a particular player — Tony Fitzpatrick from Bristol City. The first part was straightforward but the second was more tricky. I had been a strong admirer of Tony Fitzpatrick from his early days as the driving force at St Mirren when I was manager there. I had to weigh up whether I should allow St Mirren to dictate the terms of the deal or not. Common sense prevailed. The plain fact was that I believed we needed Weir to give us width and balance. I had to telephone Tony to explain the situation and he signed for St Mirren the next day. The day after that the Weir-Scanlon exchange took place. That was followed very shortly after by the departure of Duncan Davidson to the States for £18,000 — and that with a sense of sorrow for I was fond of Duncan.

Our next active period in the transfer market really followed on from our victory in the European Cup-Winners' Cup in 1983. That season brought an abrupt and tragic end to Stuart Kennedy's footballing career and meant that I had to find a full-back. We had watched Stewart McKimmie playing against us several times and in different positions with Dundee and were impressed by what we saw. We decided to run the rule over him and soon found him to have a varied range of skills. Each time we watched him something else showed — one week it would be his heading abilities, the next it would be his pace. We were becoming quite excited about the prospect of signing him and were given the unwitting help of the press in doing so. They kept writing that the Dens Park player we were interested in was Iain Ferguson, so much so that Donald McKay, the Dundee manager at the time, telephoned me to ask about the press rumours. This gave me the necessary lead to discuss McKimmie and shortly afterwards their directors visited Pittodrie and the deal was secured for £87,500 — certainly one of the best signings I have ever made.

The McKimmie deal served to highlight another aspect of the transfer market — press speculation. I always believe in keeping my business in transfers as quiet as possible beforehand, although that obviously doesn't please the football writers. What should be remembered is that you are dealing with players' livelihoods and that should always be respected.

Ironically the McKimmie deal was the last that was ever done for the Dens Park club by Donald McKay. He had travelled up to Aberdeen to discuss matters with me on one of the worst nights of weather I can remember. His anxiety was obvious as he sat in my house till the early hours talking about his problems. Despite my pleas for him to stay overnight, he was adamant about travelling back to Dundee that night. Donald was sacked the next day.

By another of those strange twists of fate, Donald McKay's successor at Dens Park was to be my assistant manager, Archie Knox, and Archie's departure from Pittodrie took me into the transfer market again when I brought Willie Garner back to Aberdeen. I had previously sold Willie to Celtic as a player for £45,000 as he was unable to command a regular place in the first team after recovering from a leg break. Another great servant also left the club around this time — old Crime Count himself, Drew Jarvie, who joined St Mirren for £2,000 and is still thriving at Love Street as player/coach.

During the summer break in 1983 I realised that although I didn't have any players whose contracts would run out until the end of the 1983-84 season, there would be problems ahead, and particularly with one player — Gordon Strachan. He had already been to see me to tell me he was becoming a bit bored with life at Aberdeen and my reaction then had been terse. I told him to go and get himself unbored and that if winning cups and medals as a footballer bored him then there must be something seriously wrong with him! But deep down I understood the kind of boredom Gordon was talking about. He is very much an individual and needs different platforms to perform on from time to time, regular fresh challenges. At least it was to his credit that he gave me plenty of warning beforehand so that I could prepare for his certain departure.

I began to look around the Scottish scene for a possible replacement and stumbled upon Billy Stark by accident. Even then, I wasn't sure if he would be available, for I had tried to bring him to Pittodrie when I became manager at Aberdeen and St Mirren had turned down my £100,000 offer then. Near the end of the 1982-83 season, in fact, Jim McLean had telephoned me to ask my evaluation of Stark and I was totally frank and honest in my assessment, just as I would expect Jim to be to me in a similar circumstance. I had brought Stark to St Mirren as a kid and had watched him develop into an excellent player with a goalscoring touch. I told Jim that Stark was possibly in something of a rut at Love Street, that he would possibly be keen to move and that he would undoubtedly be a useful acquisition if Jim could get him at the right price. Jim telephoned later to say that St Mirren had turned down his offer of £55,000 and were sticking out for over £70,000 — a price the Tannadice club were not prepared to pay. With this information in mind I telephoned the St Mirren manager, Ricky McFarlane, whom I had also brought into the Love Street set-up, and made a straight offer of £70,000. He approached his board with the news and the next day I concluded the deal. I was delighted for I knew I now had a year to get Billy Stark used to the ways of Aberdeen Football Club before the wee man left.

To make the whole transaction viable and to achieve a balance in the books, we sold Andy Watson to Leeds United. He was a player who in many ways was underestimated in the job he did for Aberdeen. In 1980, when we won our first Premier League title, Andy was a major factor in the side, bringing strength, aggression and enthusiasm to the centre midfield position and balancing out the finer skills of Strachan and McMaster. Andy had since lost his place in the team and although he was on the substitutes' bench for the European Cup-Winners' Cup Final, he obviously was not happy about being second choice to the emerging Neale Cooper and Neil Simpson. Really I had every sympathy for the lad. He had been such a good servant for the club despite occasionally taking undeserved criticism from the fans for a style which compared unfavourably with the more skilful Strachan or McMaster. Leeds United were keen to sign him and the player was keen to move. The money we received for Andy Watson paid for Billy Stark.

Billy Stark

When the 1983-84 season ended we knew Gordon Strachan was going. Under the freedom of contract rules there was no way that Aberdeen Football Club would hold him. The only real question was which club Gordon would sign for and whether it would be in Britain or Europe. Agents representing about half of the European teams I'd ever heard of all seemed to be making a bee-line for Gordon.

Roma were prominent among those showing an early interest, firstly through a football agent called Bev Walker and then through another man called Johnny Rivers. Gordon came to talk with me about that offer but eventually decided that Italian football might not be suited to his type of play. I think he possibly made a hasty decision there. Present Italian football is in such a marvellous upswing and Gordon might well have relished the marvellous platform provided there among the big names and playing in front of the big crowds.

Then Cologne started to show an interest through an agent called Killat. We had known him previously as he had helped organise one or two of our pre-season tours and he therefore knew some of the players and the directors. He was in Aberdeen a lot at that particular time and while the directors presumed that he was over to help organise another tour or something similar, he was actually away signing Gordon Strachan behind our backs. As it transpired he had convinced the player to sign a contract without our knowledge in the very team hotel we were staying in while preparing for our European semi-final against Porto! It was a totally unacceptable situation and a type of behaviour which modern football can well do without.

In fact the whole Strachan transfer saga stems largely from my decision to drop him from our team for a match against Hearts. I felt that Gordon was going through a spell in which his motivation on the field was wavering and that a slight shock would do him no harm. I never explain to the press whether I have dropped players and if they want to make an issue over a player's non-appearance that is up to them. I didn't say anything this time either.

At that time Gordon contributed a regular weekly article to the *Daily Express* in which he talked about aspects of football in an uncontentious way. There was never anything in it which could really be construed as damaging to Aberdeen Football Club and he was no doubt adequately paid for his efforts. That week, though, the headline for his column stated that Fergie was wrong and the column itself went into the reasons why he should have played. I did not react right away but the day after that I simply told him that I was withdrawing the privilege we had granted for him to write for the newspaper. That was the way I decided to handle it but inevitably it led to a falling out

Gordon Strachan scoring with a penalty

between the player and myself.

It is against this background that Gordon's rash act of signing for Cologne must be viewed. He obviously stopped coming to me for advice and just as obviously took the advice of Cologne's agent instead. It wasn't until we had agreed a deal for Gordon's transfer to Manchester United and told the player about it that he informed us he had secretly signed a contract with Cologne. He apologised sincerely and was already regretting his error, but I was thunderstruck. I said, 'What do you think you're doing going to a club like Cologne? Last year they were playing to crowds of about 3,000 in some games. You need a big platform and that's why you're leaving Aberdeen in the first place.' I told him there was no bigger platform than at Manchester United where crowds of 40,000 to 50,000 were a regular feature.

Eventually, though, we were informed that the document Gordon had signed had no legal validity and by that time no one was more relieved about that than the wee man himself. Gordon Strachan duly did the good deed and signed for Manchester United. He was happy to join one of the biggest clubs in the world and we were happy with our £500,000 transfer fee. It was then that all the problems started. Cologne complained to UEFA and the transfer was temporarily halted. It meant protracted dealings between the directors of Aberdeen, Manchester United and Cologne at venues in Paris and the south of France, but eventually the issue was settled with Aberdeen making a small payment to Cologne and Manchester United agreeing to play the German team in a friendly over there as a form of reimbursement. Gordon Strachan was at last a Manchester United player but there can have been few Old Trafford players before him who took so long to pull on the famous red strip.

At least I had been expecting Strachan's departure but the loss to Aberdeen within weeks of both McGhee and Rougvie was a shock. In fairness to Mark, he had mentioned to me some months before that he thought he would be leaving but to which club he had no idea. There was talk of Celtic and Southampton as well as the two German clubs, Hamburg and Borussia Dortmund. After the celebrations when we came back to Aberdeen with the Scottish Cup that season, I had asked Mark what his plans were. He said that he would come in and discuss the situation with me on the Monday but he knew even then that he was about to fly to Glasgow and then on to Hamburg on the Sunday. It was a disappointing end to what I felt to be a good relationship with Mark but although he could have left the club in a more honest way he was a great player for Aberdeen and his departure contributed handsomely to the club's profits.

Doug Rougvie

159

Doug Rougvie's departure to join Chelsea was perhaps the biggest shock of all. He was a lad the club had done a lot for. He was a great character about the place and had a tremendous rapport with the supporters. Although not a great player by any means, Doug was influential at Pittodrie. He was an imposing figure in a red jersey and his enthusiasm merged well with the other ingredients in the team, so much so that he became a regular first-team player who seemed to improve with each season.

When I first arrived at Pittodrie I noticed big Doug's wages were less than most of the other players and I couldn't understand it. I immediately raised his wage scale to the same standard as the rest and he rewarded the club in return. I really felt sorry for the big man on the two occasions he was sent off, one in a League Cup-tie, and the other in a Scottish League Cup Final, the latter especially so as it was an unjustified decision.

From time to time, though, Doug Rougvie had wanted to leave Aberdeen, convinced he could make more money down south. I remember once when Middlesbrough tried to sign him he was sitting in the hallway at Pittodrie with his wife at 8.30 in the morning to see me. He was desperate to get away and accused me of denying him the chance to play in English football. I told him he might well regret joining Middlesbrough anyway and events proved me right when they were relegated that year.

Nonetheless it was a disappointment how Rougvie set about leaving the club. He came to me on the first day of training for the 1984-85 season. It was a Monday morning and I had just returned from holiday on the Sunday to read reports of Chelsea's interest in him. In fact I knew previously that Chelsea had approached a journalist of my acquaintance to tap Doug Rougvie. With the newspaper reports on top of that I was more than half expecting his visit to my office. When he came in, his demands were quite blunt. If I didn't match Chelsea's offer he was leaving. I told him I'd already made him a good offer in keeping with his ability and that football wasn't only about moving for a couple of pounds extra. It was also about winning honours and bonuses came along as part of that. However, I also told him I would take up the matter with the directors at lunchtime and let him know after that. He said that would be fine.

That was the last time I saw Doug Rougvie. He jumped on a plane at lunchtime that day and the next thing I heard he was in London and had signed for Chelsea. Doug, then, was another player who did himself no favours by the manner of his departure from the club.

Anyway, with McGhee and Rougvie now gone, I had to think and

Frank McDougall waits for the half-chance

Frank McDougall scores against Coventry

act quickly. We signed Tom McQueen from Clyde. Tommy was a young full-back whom we had watched the previous season and been impressed enough to ask him to come up to Pittodrie to train. His work commitments had prevented that. Now we decided to take the chance. He was young, keen, and although he had only played football on a part-time basis we felt he could develop. At £80,000 he has turned out to be a marvellous investment for the club and had an outstanding spell in his first season at Pittodrie.

We also decided to make a move for Frank McDougall who had undoubtedly been the best striker we had played against in the past three or four seasons. Although he was a player who seemed to have some sort of problem from time to time, we felt that we could take the chance. For a payment of £100,000 to St Mirren he is another great investment. He is one of the best finishers in the game, easily on a par with Joe Harper, and a good footballer too. Hopefully the longer he is with us the better he will become.

McDougall was in fact the fifth player I brought from St Mirren to Pittodrie. First there were Dougie Bell and Steve Cowan, both signed from Love Street on free transfers. Then of course Peter Weir joined the Pittodrie set-up and finally we bought Billy Stark for £70,000 and Frank McDougall for £100,000. Flowing the other way, from Aberdeen to Paisley, were Ian Scanlon, as part of the Peter Weir transfer deal, Derek Hamilton, who joined the Saints for £4,000, and Drew Jarvie, who went to Love Street as player/coach. It seemed like the whole transfer market in microcosm, but in truth I knew most of the players at Love Street from the time I spent there, and I also reckoned I could give them the right sort of platform at Pittodrie for their particular skills.

I suppose the transfers of Steve Cowan, to Hibs for £30,000, and Doug Bell, to Rangers for £115,000, have to be considered as great deals for Aberdeen as both were discarded players from Love Street. In that sense I must confess that both deals did give me a large amount of personal satisfaction, particularly the transfer for Steve, who is perhaps not the most stylish of players but who has a great attitude to the game and who refused to give up despite a serious injury at one stage in his career. He will always hold a special place in my memory.

Doug Bell was a talented but undisciplined player in his earlier days and it took us quite a time to straighten him out. It is to his credit that he made it and I am sure he could have been one of the top players for Aberdeen, and perhaps even Scotland, if he had not sustained the injuries he did and if he had not been so insistent in refusing to change his style. There was certainly a place for Doug's individual style of play but I was keen for him to channel it through the team pattern and also to improve other aspects of his game, which I know he found difficult. Nonetheless I was disappointed in him when he asked me for a transfer and was at first reluctant to grant his request. He persisted and I relented at the end of the 1984-85 season but, as with Steve Cowan, I felt that a wee bit of Alex Ferguson was leaving too. I had brought both these boys into football at St Mirren and was proud to watch them grow in stature and ability.

My last three signings in my first seven years as manager of the Dons, though, have also given me satisfaction as well as confidence for the future. For two of them at least I must pay respect here to the excellent standard of scouting which has been developed at Aberdeen Football Club through chief scout John Carswell, who carries out his duties without fuss or recognition, and all my other scouts, as well as youth coaches, Lenny Taylor and George Adams. This system brought young midfielder Brian Grant to Pittodrie from Stirling Albion for £35,000 as well as Brian Irvine from Falkirk for £55,000. Both will be marvellous assets to the club. Jim Bett, whom we signed from Lokeren for £280,000, is of course a player of international stature and will bring a new dimension to the team.

As any manager — and more so any director — will tell you, the books have to be balanced. My past seven years at Aberdeen have certainly done that successfully, though none of that would have been possible but for the understanding of our chairman, Mr Donald, and his able directors. I know they must have been at their wit's end a few times in my transfer dealings!

Chapter Eleven
Job Offers

SUCCESS IS A marvellous feeling for any manager, especially as he is always the first one to be judged at any club. The success of the team can often determine the length of time he will be in the job. Aberdeen are something of an exceptional club in that sense — they have never had a reputation for firing managers or parting with them under mysterious circumstances. Nevertheless, the success I've had with the Dons has raised from time to time the inevitable question, 'How long will you stay at Aberdeen?'

The longer our successful run continues the more I am asked, so much so that I sometimes wonder if some people would prefer to see me leave! What many of these people overlook is that Aberdeen is a big club in every sense. Facilities are good, salaries are high and more than one manager of an English First Division club has cast an envious eye on the Aberdeen job. Nevertheless, our very success at Aberdeen has created a bit of a problem occasionally in that I have been offered other managerial positions. And the first job offer came — as it always happens — at a most inappropriate time.

I don't think there is ever a *right* time to leave a club like Aberdeen. My attitude has always been that no club has yet offered me better working conditions than this one. However, going back to 1982, prior to us playing away to Motherwell in a Scottish Cup tie, I was offered the chance to go to Wolverhampton Wanderers. Of course Wolves had a marvellous tradition of success in the early 1950s. They were one of the first British clubs to sample European football and many will remember their great matches against Honved and Moscow Dynamo. This was a big club with a big reputation, fallen on hard times. I gave the offer consideration for a day or two and decided in fairness to both them and myself to go down and meet their chairman and directors.

I must say I was totally disillusioned by what I saw at Molineux. The stadium was in a state of disrepair and there was a general air of defeat. The most amazing thing was that there was not a soul in the ground that afternoon. To me there was apathy and lack of ambition, or maybe just laziness. I couldn't believe it — a full-time professional club which had no one working in the afternoon. The lady secretary was the only form of life I saw at the ground that day.

The meeting with the directors was also disappointing. They began by asking questions about how I managed and I said, 'Look, I could give you answers to what you want to know but I thought I was down here to be offered a job, not to be asked questions from a board whose members obviously don't know anything about me.' Were they going to offer me the job or not? If so, I would then have to consider it. I made the point that I already had a good job and was not necessarily looking for another one. The directors then finished their lunch and left and the chairman remained behind. When we were alone he offered me the job. I said I would consider it, but I knew then that there was no chance of me accepting. The whole set-up was puzzling and, more importantly from my point of view, was just not on the same plain as Aberdeen.

Anyway, that offer is now history but over the last year or so it has become increasingly difficult for me in that bigger clubs have come with offers which have made me think more seriously about the whole question of moving.

I had already been approached by a Rangers director immediately after winning the European Cup-Winners' Cup and the Scottish Cup in 1983 and I had declined then. I was reluctant to even consider a move then because John Greig was still managing Glasgow Rangers and he was a good friend of mine. There was no way I was going to pull the carpet from under John's feet. When Aberdeen went to Ibrox the following season and beat Rangers 2-0, with two Mark McGhee goals, the jungle drums were beating and John was obviously under pressure. It came to a head on Saturday 22 October, after we beat Celtic 3-1 at Pittodrie. That midweek, John resigned as manager. It was a shattering experience for the man. He had obviously had enough. Immediately I received a phone call from a journalist asking me if I was interested in becoming manager of Rangers.

Next I received another call — from John Paton, then vice-chairman of Rangers, but now chairman. He spelled out what he was prepared to offer me to manage Rangers. He also turned out to be a presistent caller over the next four or five days.

Obviously the Rangers offer had to be considered seriously. This was an opportunity to manage a great club I was born and bred next door to. As a boy I was obviously Rangers daft — the most natural thing to be for almost anyone from Govan. It kept running through my mind that there had been boys from Govan who had played for

Rangers — myself among them — but no one from Govan had ever actually managed the club. Furthermore, I was not under contract to Aberdeen, although the chairman and I had spoken about me signing one. If I had chosen, I was free to do whatever I wanted. There was nothing to bind me there other than a moral obligation in that I had verbally agreed to sign a contract. In the end that was probably to be the most important factor of all: I felt I couldn't go back on my word to Aberdeen Football Club.

Many of my friends phoned me up to say that I was the right man for the Ibrox job and that I would be a fool not to take it and for two or three nights my wife and I sat up until the small hours trying to decide what was best, not just for me but for her and for the kids' education as well. It was a decision which I wrestled with deep inside. I did speak to one person for advice, and that was Scot Symon.

Scot had been my manager as a player for Rangers and was a man I had great faith in and respect for, a man who knew all about Rangers and who had in fact been sacked in a deplorable manner by them in 1967 — an action which to this day I consider the worst thing that ever happened to that club. The minute Scot Symon left Rangers, they seemed to lose their greatness. I knew he would give me honest advice. He told me I must take the job. In fact I was surprised at his conviction on the subject despite his harsh treatment by the club. His only reservation regarding my acceptance concerned the directors themselves. Who on the board of Glasgow Rangers held power at the particular time and were they the same group as was offering me the manager's place? He was able to find out some of these answers himself but when we spoke on the telephone the next evening he remained unsure about the unity of the board. His information was that two separate directors were competing for the chairman's seat.

Now, such an issue may be largely irrelevant to the ordinary football supporter and street punter but to a manager it is all-important. At the end of the day, the most important relationship in the running of a club — and particularly of a big rich club like Rangers — is between the manager and the chairman. That relationship had to be established on a firm footing from the start, otherwise the confrontation would inevitably occur and the loser, just as inevitably, would be the manager.

The media had of course built the job issue up. They were already speculating on many aspects including who my assistant would be. Some of them who don't even know my beliefs were forecasting the signing of Roman Catholics. One particular news item on Radio 2 made me absolutely livid. The journalist boomed out some stuff like,

166

'The corridors of power at Ibrox are about to be shaken to their very roots. Alex Ferguson will be manager of Rangers Football Club tomorrow and his first signing will be a Roman Catholic.' That really angered me as, for one, the man doesn't know me and secondly, I have never spoken to him on any subject far less football. Although I did discuss the religious subject with John Paton it was not an issue with me. As far as I am concerned managing footballers is all that matters and I have never had interference of any kind from my directors at Aberdeen Football Club and would expect that policy to rule no matter where I managed.

But I didn't only have to consider the Rangers job in itself, I also had to consider my position at Aberdeen, what it meant to me and what the club had done for me. The people at the club and the directors had seen me through difficult times — the time of my tribunal with St Mirren and the time of my father's death. They had consistently told me that they would have patience in waiting for success and the club had a tremendous tradition of good relationships with their managers. I began to wonder if I could expect the same backing at any other club. These were important enough issues but so was the fact that at Aberdeen I had some very good players who had signed new contracts with the club on the basis that I would be there. That was a big obligation.

It doesn't matter how many times you turn things round and stand them upside down on their head, at the end you've got to make a decision. That decision to stay with Aberdeen Football Club was taken in my solicitor's office where the new contract was drawn up. We then made the short walk to the chairman's office where it was duly signed by all parties. Drinks were then poured amidst a lot of relief from everyone, none more so than my solicitor, Les Dalgarno, and accountant, Colin Cameron, who had threatened me with backdated fees which they warned would be hefty if I moved! Many people who thought that I had made a financial killing out of the situation would be interested to know that I never asked for one penny extra from the agreement on my salary of five months previously. It was all about job satisfaction.

I then phoned John Paton in his hotel in Portugal where Rangers were playing Porto. I thanked him for his offer but told him I was staying. All he said was that he had heard and was disappointed but nonetheless wished me well.

The rest is history. Who knows whether a person is ever right or wrong in issues like this? So much of my childhood surrounded the area around Ibrox Park and my love for the club as a boy was great.

How could I forget those schoolboy days playing on the Ibrox School pitch with Bill Struth, the great man himself, watching from his window in the Stadium. Often I made sure I was playing outside-left one half and outside-right in the other half so that he had every chance of seeing me, so convinced was I that he had to sign me immediately — at 10 years of age! But when you grow up to become an adult you've got to think like an adult. That decision had to be taken not by Alex Ferguson, the Rangers-daft kid, but Alex Ferguson, the manager of Aberdeen. I now have no regrets whatsoever in turning the job down to stay with Aberdeen Football Club.

Having got that particular heart-wrenching experience out of the road, I was totally drained. We had a game that night against Beveren which worked out exceptionally well for us — a 4-0 victory — and the reception the supporters gave me was marvellous. It reminded me of a time when I was playing for Falkirk under the then manager, Willie Cunningham. Willie had been offered the job as manager of the Scottish team and, like me with the Rangers job, was anguishing over his decision. On a night when 22,000 fans packed into Brockville for a Falkirk-Hibernian League Cup tie, Willie announced his decision to stay with Falkirk over the tannoy system. The reception he got was tremendous!

The next time I was offered a job I had to think seriously about was the summer of 1984 when I was approached by Tottenham Hotspur. Now Spurs are obviously one of the big traditional clubs in England. It is a club which is now a public company with a magnificent new stand and a reputation for playing entertaining football. The recipe for that job was certainly right. I liked the principle of the way the club was run in the sense that they admired pure football and that to me was a big incentive. Having spoken to Irving Scholar, the chairman, I was impressed also by his enthusiasm for the club.

After many telephone calls with Irving and a meeting with the self-made millionaire himself along with another Spurs director, Paul Bobroff, we were down to discussion of wages, conditions and housing, which all seemed perfectly acceptable. We even discussed players and in particular Steve Archibald. Irving agreed with me that Steve should stay with Spurs and that I would get more out of him as a player. But the one grey area that worried me was the length of contract Spurs were prepared to offer — originally a two-year deal when I would have wanted five years. They later improved that to three years but I was not convinced that was long enough to do the job.

Once again I opted to stay with Aberdeen. However I will say that I was impressed by Irving Scholar, with all his ideas and infectious enthusiasm. He certainly made a mark on me. Some of his lighter moments in our various telephone discussions featured his fascination for football quizzes. Of course I'm reasonably good at this type of thing and he was always trying to catch me out on a number of trick football questions. He'll have to buy another book before he'll do that!

From time to time, however, a person does need fresh challenges. I was fortunate at this period to be offered the Scotland assistant manager's job. After consultation with Jock Stein himself and with the Aberdeen directors, I decided to accept the offer to assist him with the preparation of the pool for the forthcoming World Cup ties. It was an obvious challenge for me. I had been six years with the club and felt I could afford the time, and with Aberdeen being knocked out early in the European Cup and in our domestic League Cup it worked out fine. Anyway there would be a lot of midweek international games at both full and Under-21 level when I would have several players away training with the national squads and would have been left at home in Aberdeen twiddling my thumbs for much of the time. So the challenge came at the right moment and provided me with the opportunity to see how the operation works at that level.

Working with men like Dalglish and Souness has broadened my outlook on top players and how to handle them. It is all very well dealing with your normal club players but you read so much about the Souness's and the Dalglish's and the Nicholas's, and until you go to work with them you don't have any concept of how they themselves react, how they behave, how they train, what they think of the game. That experience has been invaluable.

The hardest part of the Scotland job, in fact, as with running any international side, is the lack of time you have to spend with players. No sooner is the game over than you are shaking hands with them, wishing them good luck for their club matches on the Saturday and arranging to see them again in three months' time or whenever the next international fixture is due. The situation becomes especially difficult after a bad result for the Scotland team, like the one we had at Hampden against Wales in the World Cup qualifying section. To have had the players staying overnight after the match and to be able to thrash the problems out with them the next day would have been invaluable. But clubs take priority, the players have their duties to their clubs and the clubs have responsibilities to their supporters.

I have been genuinely amazed at the enormity of the Scottish manager's job. The most difficult task of all, in fact, is choosing the team and the main problem there is who exactly to leave out. You only have to look at the number of really good players in any Scottish squad to realise that fact. I always make a point of telling the ones left out that in a way they are more important than those picked to play, for their very presence in the squad prevents anyone from becoming complacent.

Alan Hansen is a good case in point. In most people's eyes Alan is one of the most complete players in Britain and yet he cannot get his place in the Scottish team because of the Alex McLeish and Willie Miller partnership. If you examine their defensive record in season 1984-85 for Scotland you will find that in six international matches the pair conceded only four goals and that alone warrants their inclusion at the expense of others. Gordon Strachan is another exceptionally skilled player who has had to be patient waiting for his international recall because of the consistent performances from McStay, Souness and Bett. Even more of a problem for any Scottish manager is the choice of strikers from among the capable bunch of Dalglish, Johnston, Nicholas, Sturrock, Archibald, Sharp, Speedie and Gray. Despite these problems every member of the Scottish squad has been quite selfless and it is clear that they are all Scots and proud of it.

A prime example again is Dave Speedie of Chelsea who has impressed me perhaps more than anyone in 1985. His attitude in the squad has been magnificent. When he was chosen against England he was so excited and showed a commendable sense of humour when the other lads joked with him about his Sassenach accent. He did well in that match and had every right to think that he would also be chosen for the following midweek World Cup match in Iceland. Jock Stein and I, though, felt that Gray and Sharp were the right combination for that particular match, and Speedie's reaction to their selection and his obvious willingness and delight in simply being part of the squad, reflected well upon him. That kind of team spirit is all-important. Again, when Speedie was selected for the important World Cup match at Cardiff and many people were questioning his explosive temperament, he came through with flying colours. His performance was a decisive factor in that game.

Another player in the Scotland squad that I have a lot of confidence in is Charlie Nicholas. I, like many people, expected Charlie to be the unofficial King of London by now, for there hasn't been a player since Jim Baxter in Scotland who has caught my imagination more than Charlie. It has been a disappointment to me and to Scotland that Charlie has not really produced the goods yet since his move to Arsenal.

I remember Terry Neill, when he was manager at Highbury, telephoning me one morning to ask my opinion of Charlie and I almost begged Terry to sign him. Of course some people would say that Charlie's departure from Celtic would obviously suit Aberdeen Football Club and they would be right, but if a fellow manager asks an opinion of a player he has a right to hear the whole truth. If I go to John Lyall or David Pleat or Bob Paisley for advice, as I have done in the past, then I expect their opinion to be an honest one. When Terry phoned me I waxed lyrical about the lad.

The aspect that impressed me most about Charlie was not the fact that he scored goals but the variety of goals that he scored. He was two-footed, could beat a man, had good balance and composure on the ball, good vision and was one of the few players who could score from outside the box by creating a foot of space to get a shot in. I told Terry Neill that I believed Charlie would become a really great player and I still think that he can. Like so many young players who have a meteoric rise to stardom he has to come to terms with living in a huge goldfish bowl, being a constant centre of attraction. I will be surprised if he doesn't manage that part, for having worked with him in the Scotland set-up, I have found him to be bright, imaginative and intelligent — qualities which should encourage responsibility in his tasks as a player.

Generally speaking my association with the Scotland squad — Anglos and home players alike — has been excellent and I have really enjoyed the involvement. Two particular highlights stand out for me from that year working under Jock Stein. The first was Kenny Dalglish's goal at Hampden in the World Cup against Spain. It was straight out of the top drawer of class and ingenuity. Kenny manoeuvred his body and the ball to give himself just a look at goal and executed the shot in the way we have seen him do so often. To me his sheer skill in manufacturing that extra half a foot of space in order to get his shot in was an important highlight of an exciting year.

The other source of great satisfaction in that year, however, was to be involved in beating England. Although it wasn't a pretty game, our team battled well in difficult conditions and, apart from a 15-minute spell in the second-half when England turned the screws on, we were always in control.

But the abiding memory for me in my time with the Scottish team was the sheer presence of Jock Stein. To have worked with Jock is to me an honour beyond description. The tragedy of his death hit us all with a sickening thump, but just how much it affected other people is difficult for me to equate with my own feelings. Never since my father's death have I felt the way I did that week and the same recriminations I felt when my father died resurfaced. Did I do enough for him? I keep telling myself that I should have read the signs earlier.

171

He was obviously not feeling well after half-time in that game against Wales in Cardiff but, typical of the man, he never said a word. When we scored our equaliser from a penalty everyone else leaped off the bench to cheer except Jock and it was then, when I came to my seat and patted Jock on the head, that I should have known. He just sat motionless and I didn't read into that the meaning that I should have because my thoughts were totally absorbed in a stupid game of football.

There are many memories of Jock Stein which will be everlasting because of his exceptional life but there were particular aspects of him that separated him from ordinary mortals and made him something special. In my years of association with him never once did he raise the subject of his achievements — not a mention of his triumph in Lisbon, or his winning nine League titles in a row. There were many times when I was inquisitive about his successes but although obviously proud, he never broached the subject himself and quickly dismissed it if I did. His humility was, as in the case of my father, so important to him.

In Hugh McIlvanney's tribute to him in *The Observer* he emphasised the part the mining community played in Jock's life and the big man never forgot it. I remember during the miners' strike when we were travelling from Turnberry to Hampden for home games, if we passed a lorry carrying coal and obviously strike-breaking Jock would be less than pleased. His commitment to his own people was total.

My most lasting memory of a truly remarkable man is of Jock turning to me at one point during the second-half of the game in Cardiff and saying, 'Let's not lose our dignity. Whatever the result, we must keep our dignity.' Considering the responsibility on his shoulders and the importance of that one game for him, that was a sentiment which captured the very essence of the man. The result that night gave Scotland the chance of qualifying for the World Cup Finals for the fourth time in a row — a remarkable achievement for a small country like ours. I would hope that the Scotland players, irrespective of who is in charge, will respond to the leadership and spirit which Jock Stein bequeathed them.

Chapter Twelve
Referees

IT HAS TO be said that in my early years at Love Street and Pittodrie I was not exactly the mildest of managers as far as referees were concerned. I have since learned that, although as a manager you are obviously under extreme pressure in matches, it simply doesn't pay to confront referees about their decisions. In fairness to managers, however, we often get disillusioned with the Report System that operates as a means of assessing a referee's performance. Often little or nothing is done about it when reports criticising a referee are submitted. Part of the problem, of course, is that it is usually the losing manager who complains and his objections can therefore be dismissed as little more than a case of sour grapes.

I have been banned from the touchline twice in my time as manager at Aberdeen. The first was brought about in a match against St Mirren at Paisley on 25 February 1979 — the day my father died. I'll never forget it. We had travelled down and spent the Friday night in a hotel and on the Saturday morning someone tipped me off that St Mirren had called in the referee for a ground inspection due to the weather conditions. Obviously, the last thing we would have wanted would have been for the match to be called off. I arrived at Love Street just as the referee and the St Mirren manager were having a chat in the tunnel. The referee had already completed his inspection and was not happy with the state of the ground. I immediately took a look for myself and found the pitch surprisingly good. I pointed out to the referee that there were only two valid reasons for the game being called off — either that there was a danger to the players or that the markings on the pitch and touchlines were indistinguishable. He was immediately aggressive towards me and let me know that he, not I, was the referee and that he would make the decision.

The game did go ahead and in fact ended in a 2-2 draw after we had been ahead by two goals. In the first-half, though, I was unhappy with some of the referee's decisions and went to his room at half-time to ask him about them. He immediately said he was reporting me to the SFA.

I couldn't believe it. I had simply requested his permission to ask him a question — and I'm still waiting to ask it! But to my mind there was no question that his control over the game was questionable. By the end of that match he had booked seven Aberdeen players and then sent off Ian Scanlon and Willie Miller towards full-time — those statistics, to me, were a terrible indictment on Aberdeen Football Club. When the referee's report went to the SFA it included an accusation that I had lunged at him in the tunnel at the end of the game and while a saint himself might have contemplated such an action, that part of his report was simply not true. Plenty of witnesses, as well as my own directors, would testify to the fact that I never at any time attempted to speak to the referee or even go near him after the game. Anyway, I was banned from the touchline and fined.

My second offence took place on 5 May 1980, the day Aberdeen won the Premier League for the first time. I had words with the referee, Brian McGinlay, at half-time for I felt that Steve Archibald should be given more protection. I reacted badly and shouldn't have pursued the matter. I thought that Brian McGinlay would have let me have my say and then get on with it. I was wrong and that incident was the only blot on an otherwise great day for the club. I have regretted those words ever since.

No one needs to tell me how hard a referee's job is. I wouldn't take their place for a million pounds. I've said time and time again that football referees are paid far too little. I have also consistently argued for a two-tier system of refereeing, where one group of referees is totally in control of Premier League matches — referees who have been proven and tested in bigger matches in front of big crowds. In order to prevent this top group of referees becoming complacent there should be in the lower tier a number of younger referees as well as experienced men who have been found wanting in their control of the bigger matches but who could handle most first and second division matches. This idea has been mooted by many people in the game over the years and it amazes me that the system has never changed. The referees in the lower tier should have chances of promotion, just as the football clubs have from division to division. If a referee has had consistently bad reports from clubs and supervisors alike, then he should be demoted. Similarly if there are two or three referees from the lower grade who have obviously performed well, then they should be promoted. That is a logical system, one in which referees would be made to pay for bad performances in the same way as players do week in, week out.

I still maintain that Brian McGinlay has easily been Scotland's best

Counting them out?

referee over the last ten or fifteen years and the natural successor to Bob Davidson, who in my playing days was easily best. Brian McGinlay outshines everyone among the present crop of referees but there are times that even he has off days and a major part of this problem with referees is surely motivation. How can you expect a man who is used to controlling European ties or International games or Old Firm matches one week to have the same motivation for travelling to Forfar or Brechin or Cowdenbeath to take charge of a match there on a wet and dirty Wednesday night in front of 300 or 400 people? Inconsistency is almost bound to occur in a bad system. My sympathy goes out to top referees like McGinlay, Bob Valentine, Gordon Smith and Alan Ferguson in a situation like this as they are good referees with plenty of experience.

Valentine, incidentally, is another referee I admire, largely because he enjoys his football. He makes sure he is 100% fit and prepared for the game. It is often quite clearly seen that we have a number of referees who are not physically fit enough to referee Premier Division matches and that is an indictment on our refereeing system. The supervisors must do more to ensure that the standard of fitness among the men who control the games on the park is higher than we've seen over the recent years. It's got to be borne in mind that the speed of the game and the fitness standard of the players have improved dramatically. With the increasing financial stakes in the game it is important that one aspect we can improve on — the standard of fitness among referees — should be adhered to.

My one-year ban in 1980 kept me away from the touchline even in European games. It was a big wrench for me really. I love to be involved with my team, especially in the second-half. I do have regrets. My behaviour then stemmed from the fact that I was still a young manager. I had quit playing football at 32 and at 37 years of age I was banned for a year — at an age when some players are still playing. A lot of energy I maybe should have been expending on the park was then being channelled into giving referees the benefit of my thoughts — loud and clear! Experience has since taught me to stay away from referees.

I've also realised, though, that some referees just don't have the capacity to handle a situation where they're being asked questions about decisions in the game. No one can be always right. Referees must realise that managers' lives and players' livelihoods are wrapped up in these games and it is not so unreasonable for a manager to ask questions at half-time. If the manager, the directors, the players, the press and the public cannot understand a particular decision in a match, why should we all be kept in the dark about it? The game is big enough to accept such a change and to allow referees to speak out about controversial incidents. Above all it is important to keep the public informed and involved and it should be borne in mind here that we are talking about a public that has many attractions vying for its attention against football.

Frankly, I have spoken to some referees at half-time — David Syme, Kenny Hope, Alan Ferguson — and they have been reasonable. There is absolutely no harm done. The manager comes away clear in his own mind on why a decision was taken and it works to increase the respect felt towards referees for giving him the time and explaining to him. That is very important. Referees must get respect from managers and players — if they have that they will probably find that they will in fact be questioned less.

Over a season you can only hope that refereeing inconsistencies will even themselves out. History obviously tells us that in a game at Celtic Park or Ibrox the home team are always going to get more than their even share of the breaks and I don't suppose that will ever really change. In a situation where 40,000 people are screaming at most refereeing decisions it can be difficult to give a decision against the overwhelming tide. The human element will always be there.

Chapter Thirteen
Football Managers

FOOTBALL MANAGERS really are a breed apart. Their lives are usually totally dominated by football and the pressures on them to do well with their club are heightened by the frequency of sackings in the profession. To some extent, then, they need each other's support and understanding. There have been times, for instance, when I have felt particularly depressed — after a bad European result or whatever — and needed to pick up the telephone and speak to someone who will understand because they have been in that state themselves. At other times I've been the one who is handing out the encouragement.

Jim McLean is a man whom I admire greatly as a manager. Our friendship goes back twenty years, when we shared a room at an SFA coaching school in Largs, but it is a relationship with a double edge to it. Because of the great rivalry between our two clubs we are each of us, as managers, desperate to come out on top. I never go near Jim after a game and he never comes near me. Perhaps two or three days later, when tempers have calmed, we will talk to one another about general aspects of football, though we would seldom ever discuss the previous Aberdeen-Dundee United clash.

People often criticise Jim McLean for his intensity but I can find little fault with a man who has worked as hard in football and made the sacrifices of family life and normal living that Jim was. And although he is renowned for his lack of humour I've seen Jim laugh many a time. I remember one April Fool's Day I phoned him. He was immediately suspicious and made a crack that if this had been a serious call I would have reversed the charges. I told him I hadn't even realised what day it was and went on to talk about a rearranged reserve match we were due to play. The conversation moved on to more general matters and then Jim asked me whether I'd contacted the scout which I'd promised to get him in the Glasgow area. I gave him the name of a Mr Lyon, together with a Glasgow telephone number, then rang off. Wee Jim went straight off and telephoned the Glasgow number. He was immediately connected to Calderpark Zoo! After he had cooled down he called me and told me that he'd had to admit his embarrassment to his assistant, Walter Smith, and his players before anyone from Aberdeen Football Club had a chance to tell them. That, though, is the type of kidology which goes on between us. At the end of the day it is a healthy relationship based on mutual respect for each other's achievements.

Obviously, I have also enjoyed a great relationship with the managers of the Old Firm teams over the past seven years. John Greig, in particular, has been a great pal of mine since our playing days at Ibrox. Everyone in the Rangers set-up admired John as a player. His spirit was a great force in the team and I can remember him playing so often with injuries that would sideline just about any other person. At one time he even played with both ankles strapped and while suffering from a kidney complaint. John, though, is a character with a great sense of fun as well. Going back to our Rangers days, I remember going out to celebrate a good victory in Yugoslavia with John and Dave Smith. The three of us ended up in a nightclub where the band was wearing traditional Yugoslavian dress. It didn't take us long to persuade the members of the band that we were no mean singers ourselves and soon they were donning our Rangers ties while we were donning their fancy dress. The revelry came to a sudden halt, though, when the voice of Matt Taylor, Rangers chairman at the time, boomed out from the darkness, beckoning John to come hither and the three of us to be gone!

As a manager John was always the total gentleman and would even make a point of congratulating us on our performance against them if they had lost, despite the fact that most of our games were toughly contested affairs and never short of incident. I remember one game at Ibrox in particular, when John McMaster was trodden on by Willie Johnston. Because of my respect for John Greig I refused to be drawn into comment after the game, but now that John has left Ibrox and the heat is out of the situation, I can honestly state that I believe Johnston's act that day to have been a disgusting one for any professional footballer to have carried out. But for our physiotherapist's rapid intervention I wouldn't like to think what could have happened to John McMaster.

John Greig in fact had been so courteous in defeat — we had beaten Rangers five times in season 1979-80 — that when they beat us in the semi-final of the Scottish Cup that year, I expressed my hope at a press conference after the game that Rangers would go on to lift the Cup itself. Their opponents in the Final were to be Celtic and the following Monday night, when I visited Celtic Park for a reserve game, a certain

Celtic director was ready and waiting for me to let me know in a most abrasive and aggressive fashion what he thought about my declaration of support for Rangers. Although I pointed out to him that my motives for supporting Rangers were based purely on my personal wishes for John Greig's success, the heat was only taken out of the incident by the interruption of Billy McNeill who told me there was a telephone call for me in his office. When we got to Billy's room he apologised for the director's outburst. Incidents like that, though, really bring home the prevalence of bigotry and rivalry between the Old Firm teams. If you praise Rangers then you must also praise Celtic and if you criticise one you must also criticise the other.

Billy McNeill, of course, had been manager of Aberdeen immediately before me. He is a natural leader with a good presence amongst his players and he also deals very comfortably with the press. Billy and I had always had great battles against each other as players when he was centre-half with the Parkhead side and I was centre-forward with Dunfermline and Rangers, and I used to look forward to those confrontations with the big man because although they were always tough, equally they were always fair.

It has to be said, though, that as managers we did not exactly hit it off in our early days. The fact that Billy had preceded me at Pittodrie always gave Aberdeen-Celtic matches a slight edge of intensity. Added to that was the fact that we are both bad losers. The chemistry between us during matches was explosive and from time to time the confrontations were heated, with anything but friendly exchanges firing across the dugout area. In fact Celtic's trainer, Neil Mochan, used to sit at matches and shake his head and laugh at our antics. Another time, when we were both in the directors' box, Billy and I ended up shouting at each other. After the game, when we would be enjoying a lager, Neil Mochan used to say that we were both mad, but in the heat of the moment, when two such similar temperaments clashed, it was fortunate that all that occurred were arguments.

The nature of both McNeill's and Greig's departures from the Old Firm served to remind me of what a good relationship I have with the board at Pittodrie. Billy McNeill's departure from Parkhead generated a huge amount of press attention and served to change many people's image of the Celtic board. Ironically in a way, Billy and I had only recently buried the hatchet and were actually getting on well by that time. We had many long discussions that season and it was clear that he was disillusioned with what was going on at Parkhead. He wasn't enjoying the best of relationships with his directors and the anxiety

and strain on him because of that was evident. His leaving of Parkhead
was a sad day for Scottish football because Celtic was always his great
love. The fact that he had left one of the best jobs — the Aberdeen job —
in the first place underlined that point. Celtic lost a great servant but
I'm sure now that the move to Manchester City was the best thing to
happen to Billy McNeill. Although nothing could replace his love for
Celtic, he has found a fresh challenge at Maine Road and one in which
he has already proved to be a great success. As they say, bad losers don't
often lose too often.

I remember speaking to David Hay when he first took over as
manager of Celtic. He told me that he wasn't going to let the job get on
top of him. Now he admits that the Celtic job is very much his life and
that that is inevitable when you become manager of such a big club
with a big tradition. David has found out what Billy McNeill, and every
other good manager, knows: football comes first.

John Greig's departure from Ibrox naturally led to a great deal of
speculation as to his successor and even to approaches by the Rangers
board to both myself and Jim McLean. In a way though it was apt that
Jock Wallace should end up returning to the club which has meant so
much to him. Jock, of course, is something of a legend in his own time
and is renowned as being a hard taskmaster, particularly when he puts
his lads through their pre-season paces on the Gullane sands. He
portrays that image well but those of us who know him also know a
softer side to the man. His consideration for others was well illustrated
to me when, during his first stint as manager at Ibrox and while I was
in charge of St Mirren, he telephoned me to give me encouragement at
a time when the team were going through a bad spell. He said he knew
I would be banging my head against the desk, but if I thought I had
problems I should pay a visit to Ibrox to see what problems meant. I
appreciated Jock Wallace for making that call and I still appreciate the
man.

Despite the pressures and competitiveness of the Premier League
at the end of the day the clubs and the managers have got to live with
one another and I would say that there have been relatively few
instances of blow-ups between managers during or after games. In fact
some of the so-called 'blow-ups' have had more than an element of
humour and mickey-taking to them than the public would ever
imagine. Bobby Watson, a very good friend of mine who used to
manage Airdrie until the club offered him such a raw deal that he was
forced to leave, was a good example of a character who always brought
humour to the game. He was remarkable in his absolute refusal to bow
down to the seriousness of the pressures which so many managers

Talking with Jock Wallace

succumb to and which affect so many managers' personalities. At Aberdeen we have a saying, 'I'm heading for the harbour', if things are going badly. Well, in one of our matches down at Airdrie, in which we were giving them a mother and father of a hiding, we had just scored our seventh goal when Bobby leaned out of his dugout and shouted to me, 'Excuse me, sir, could you give me the directions to the harbour?'

That kind of humour typifies Bobby. I remember another instance before a match against Airdrie. Archie Knox, Bobby Watson and I were sitting having a cup of tea in the small office opposite the Pittodrie dressing rooms when Bobby stood up and announced he was going to have a team talk. He left the door ajar, knowing full well we could hear everything that was being said, and then began by saying, 'I get the decided impression that this mob think they can take the piss out of us.' He continued at great length about making this game a war and by this time Archie and I were rolling in laughter. Bobby then came out and, straight-faced, asked us if we would have a word with our lads about allowing protection for his ball players. I, of course, reminded him that he was a lay preacher in the church and that his language and attitude could hardly be described as Christian. It was all great stuff, and it also illustrates that the demands of the job do not necessarily detract from the close bonds between managers. That spirit is emphasised any time either Jock Wallace or Frank Connor arrive at Pittodrie and are immediately greeted with the fond welcome, 'Hello, Ugly'!

The game is full of characters, at managerial level as well as any other, and no person fits that description better than Ally McLeod. Ally is still revered in Aberdeen, simply because he brought hope and optimism to the club at a time when it was badly needed. When he arrived at Pittodrie in 1975 he beat the drum to such an extent that everyone believed the team could climb Everest with their slippers on. After he won the League Cup with Aberdeen in 1976 he accepted the post of Scotland team manager and led the supporters on such a helter-skelter of euphoria that he had everyone believing we could actually win the World Cup in Argentina. It is history now how it all fell flat for the man and the viciousness of one or two members of the press brought home to everyone the fact that the fine line between becoming the biggest national hero since Rabbie Burns and being discarded as a disaster is painfully fine indeed.

I had an insight into Ally's methods when I played my last year under him at Ayr United, and even then he had that indefinable quality of sheer enthusiasm. Ally would simply never lie down in the face of adversity and that fact has been proved amply by his persistence in coming back into football management after the personal humiliation of 1978. He remains completely irrepressible. When Airdrie beat Aberdeen in the League Cup in 1984 I couldn't help but smile at Ally's reaction to the final whistle. It was sheer ecstasy. Although it was an uncomfortable feeling for me in particular, having to walk that famous gauntlet at Broomfield back to the dressing room, I was actually happy for Ally because, after all his suffering, he won his own World Cup Final that night.

Despite all that happned in Argentina, though, Ally has never lost the impish humour which has been his trademark. I remember when I played for Ayr against Aberdeen Ally used to wait for Bobby Clark to arrive, to remind him that big Alex 'Dixie' Ingram was coming for him. In fact it had become quite a battle between those two former Queen's Park players over the years and one in which the goalkeeper had to put up with a considerable amount of abuse. Ally, though, loved trying to upset Bobby Clark and when we played against Ayr in the League Cup in 1978 he made another attempt to do so by providing us with practice balls which had been soaked beforehand and were so soft that we may as well have used a haggis to kick around! During that particular game the linesman reported Ally to referee Brian McGinlay who summoned the Ayr manager to him and warned him as to his future behaviour. Ally then proceeded to spend the rest of the match standing at the tunnel entrance leaning on top of his dugout and giving the linesman stick every time he turned his back. The poor man could hardly pay attention to the game for trying to catch Ally out.

Ally left Ayr to join Motherwell some weeks later and towards the end of that season we travelled down to play at Fir Park. Again he was performing his act with the linesman until the official could take no more and started to walk over to the Motherwell dugout. Ally immediately shouted over to me, 'For God's sake, Alex, watch yourself. You can't shout like that to the linesman.' I was dumbstruck and so was the poor linesman who stopped dead in his tracks and was left wondering what to do. That's Ally, though — irrepressible to the end.

Some of the managers in the smaller clubs in Scotland do a great job and never really get the praise they deserve. Doug Houston has done very well at both Brechin and Forfar and he and I have a very good relationship, having been brought up together in Govan and having both played in the same Scottish Youth team as well as the same Queen's Park side. He too has a marvellous relationship with his chairman, Sam Smith. Craig Brown at Clyde and Alex Smith at Stirling are another two managers I have a tremendous respect for. Managers of clubs that size have extremely difficult jobs to perform. It's a continual process of selling the good players and then having to rebuild a team. In the case of Brown and Smith it is obvious from the length of time each has been in the manager's seat that their directors appreciate just what a good job they're doing for their clubs. Maybe they will never win titles and trophies the way Aberdeen have but there are different yardsticks of success. Often enough simply keeping a small club afloat and retaining the supporters it has is a greater achievement than the winning of medals and cups.

My dealings with managerial counterparts in England are obviously not as regular as in Scotland, nonetheless I have established a good relationship with most of them, especially after big midweek matches which I have flown down to see. Last season, for instance, Jock Stein and I went to Liverpool to see a sparkling performance by Everton against Bayern Munich. After the match Jock suggested that we should pop into Howard Kendall's office for a few minutes to congratulate him and wish Everton all the best in the Final. When we arrived the office was mobbed and the guest list was like a *Who's Who* of modern football. A few minutes turned into a few hours of refreshing chat about football. The same kind of thing happens at Liverpool's ground as well, where club secretary Peter Robinson always reminds me to come down and see the staff in the famous boot room where they congregate after matches.

One English manager whom I have a lot of time for and who is very different from his media image is Ron Atkinson of Manchester United. Ron has always been first-class to deal with and always makes himself available when I call the training ground or the stadium. A lot of people tend to think of him only as a flashy dresser with a liking for champagne but those who know him realise there's a lot more to the man. Certainly I've seen him with a glass of champagne after a game but I've never yet seen him finish it. In fact the main impression I get from Ron is that he's a football fanatic who will chat and argue about the game till the cows come home. He is authoritative and well-informed about the game and the players in it and it wouldn't surprise me at all if Ron's Manchester United side become one of the great teams in the club's illustrious history.

John Lyall is another English manager who is a great friend from the 1982 World Cup in Spain. The Lyall family stayed at the same apartment complex as the Fergusons. We telephone each other regularly and if I go down to London to watch a match, his scout, Charlie Faulkener, picks me up and takes me to the ground. I keep telling John that if he or his assistant at West Ham, Eddie Baily, are ever coming up to Aberdeen to give me advance warning so that I can get the squatters out of Balmoral to make way for them!

One interesting fact about John Lyall, though, is his liking for Scottish players and he often points to the number of Scots in the great English sides to have won anything. Although John is himself a Londoner his father was a Scots policeman, so it may well be that he has a surplus of Scotia's blood running through him when he makes that judgement. However he certainly picked a winner in his recent visit to Scotland when he landed the signature of Frank McAvennie, a player I am absolutely certain will prove another outstanding addition to English football.

As a matter of fact I had repeatedly tried to sign McAvennie for Aberdeen since 1983 but St Mirren simply refused to sell him to me, pointing out that I'd had my fair share of St Mirren players in recent years, with Bell, Cowan, Weir, Stark and McDougall all having come from Love Street to Pittodrie. I felt that their attitude was petty and argued that a player is either available or he's not. Anyway, I had to reconcile myself with the thought that you can't win them all, but I do know that McAvennie would have improved our side to the extent that anything would have been possible with him in an Aberdeen shirt. He is hungry, quick, brave and intelligent and will always score goals. If McAvennie can keep his feet on the ground in his new London lifestyle I think he'll prove an absolute bargain at the price and could well become the most outstanding of the Scots who have gone south in recent years. Certainly, with John Lyall behind him he's off to a great start.

Although I was delighted for John Lyall over that transfer, the one person I did feel extremely sorry for was Luton manager David Pleat, who had been chasing Frank McAvennie's signature even earlier than I had. But that loss won't stop Luton Town doing well under David, who is an exceptionally nice man with a great footballing brain. David Pleat knows exactly what he wants and, more importantly, also knows how to get it — attributes necessary in any good manager the world over.

Postscript

I HAVE TRIED to make this book as factual as possible, recording the great moments as well as the disappointments. I have also tried not to be too subjective but that has proved difficult. After all, the seven years recaptured here have been seen through my eyes and recalled through my memory.

I do feel that my time at Pittodrie has been well worthwhile. Although it has been hard work it has also been a very satisfying time for me. It is rewarding as well to look back over the years and reflect on attitudes at the time and on how the club has been run, even how I, like the players, have developed.

Trying to analyse my relative success as a manager is very difficult. People say that I'm a bad loser and that probably sums me up pretty well, but at the same time I've always been a bad loser and that didn't win me many honours or medals as a player. I do feel, though, that my upbringing has helped me. I have a devoted mother who has sacrificed a great deal of her life for my brother Martin and myself, and my father, who unfortunately did not live to see all those successes with Aberdeen, was a great influence on the kind of person I am today. It was always brought home to me in my upbringing to retain a humility and to be as natural as possible. That has helped me in my adult life.

How and when it all fitted into place I really don't know but I do think that luck and fate play their part. If asked what I regard as the vital ingredients of management I would list the ability to assess, to judge and to act without hesitation as prime factors. Players will always detect any sign of hesitance or uncertainty and it leads to a lack of confidence in a manager. But pehaps the most important guideline as a basis for success as a manager is, quite simply, to be positive.

The other important factors are being able to weigh up a player, balance a team through your selection of the right players, and, not least of all, to be able to assess yourself, critically if necessary. These should provide a firm basis for anyone entering management, but even then, to be successful you need your share of luck and your willingness to sacrifice a large chunk of your personal life for the game. All the top managers have had to make that kind of sacrifice.

Finally, my last few words in this book are for the players who have served me and Aberdeen Football Club with all the dedication and sacrifice needed. My eternal thanks go to them. Reading back through this book, though, I do notice that one unintentional and important aspect comes to light. My lack of individual recognition for Willie Miller throughout the book stems from the fact that he is such an influence and a talent in the team that he tends to be taken for granted. The magnitude of his importance to this club of ours deserves a book all to itself. Willie Miller is the only defender I have ever come across in Scottish football whom I would label as truly 'great'. I am sure every player at Pittodrie would agree — no mean praise as they themselves are a credit to the game of football.